Praise for
Bending the Arc

"Keeda Haynes suffered a great injustice, struggled, overcame it, and devoted her life to fighting against a criminal justice system responsible for tremendous harm. This is a timely and inspiring book about a subject that could not be more important."

—ERIC SCHLOSSER, *New York Times*–
bestselling author of *Fast Food Nation*

"Heartrending and heartwarming. Haynes exposes the deep flaws in our justice system, all the while exemplifying the importance of second chances."

—AUSTIN CHANNING BROWN, *New York Times*–
bestselling author of *I'm Still Here*

"A rallying story of horrific injustice and inspiring perseverance. Haynes's account of wrongful imprisonment will ignite you into action."

—VALARIE KAUR, filmmaker and author of *See No Stranger*

"The combination of lived experience with frontline legal expertise creates a riveting story that speaks directly to how we confront the racist underpinnings of mass incarceration by placing humanity and community first."

—AMY FETTIG, executive director of The Sentencing Project

"Keeda Haynes is strong, smart, and resilient. The story of her life is inextricably tied with an examination of our flawed justice system from nearly every possible angle. I came to know Haynes as a gifted and passionate advocate. I now know her to be a terrific writer. Read *Bending the Arc*."

—KEVIN RING, president of Families
Against Mandatory Minimums

"More than a coming-of-age story, *Bending the Arc* takes readers on a journey through the US criminal justice system. Haynes's book is filled with heartbreak, triumph, and resilience, offering an intimate portrait of a criminal justice system that is callous and fueled by systemic racism, patriarchy, and class hierarchy. Her survival is a testament to familial bonds, community members, and allies in the legal profession who believed in second-chance opportunities and the continued struggle for freedom and justice."

—SEKOU FRANKLIN, associate professor of political science, Middle Tennessee State University

"In *Bending the Arc*, attorney-activist Keeda Haynes scribes new stanzas, in registers of resistance, of cages, courts, community, and courage. No mere coming-of-age tale of adversity and triumph, her story testifies to the collective power of Black women nurturing, sustaining us towars new incarnations of justice."

—DR. PHYLLIS HILDRETH, vice president for institutional strategy and academics, American Baptist College

BENDING
THE
ARC

BENDING THE ARC

My Journey from Prison to Politics

KEEDA J. HAYNES

SEAL
PRESS

NEW YORK

Cover design by Kimberly Glyder
Cover images © Tawat Kambum / Shutterstock.com; © Michal Sanca / Shutterstock.com
Cover copyright © 2021 Hachette Book Group, Inc.

Seal Press
Hachette Book Group
1290 Avenue of the Americas, New York, NY 10104
www.sealpress.com
@sealpress

Printed in the United States of America
First Edition: November 2021

Published by Seal Press, an imprint of Perseus Books, LLC, a subsidiary of
Hachette Book Group, Inc. The Seal Press name and logo is a trademark
of the Hachette Book Group.

The Hachette Speakers Bureau provides a wide range of authors for speaking events.
To find out more, go to www.hachettespeakersbureau.com or call (866) 376-6591.

Names and identifying characteristics of some individuals have been changed. Where
dialogue appears, the intention was to recreate the essence of conversations rather than
verbatim quotes.

Print book interior design by Linda Mark

Library of Congress Cataloging-in-Publication Data
Names: Haynes, Keeda J., author.
Title: Bending the arc : my journey from prison to politics / Keeda J. Haynes.
Description: First edition. | New York : Seal Press, 2021.
Identifiers: LCCN 2021013553 | ISBN 9781541646308 (hardcover) |
  ISBN 9781541646292 (ebook)
Subjects: LCSH: Haynes, Keeda J. | Women ex-convicts—Tennessee—Biography. |
  African American women—Tennessee—Biography. | Public defenders—Tennessee—
  Biography. | African American women lawyers—Tennessee—Biography. | Criminal
  justice, Administration of—Tennessee. | Discrimination in criminal justice
  administration—United States. | African American women political candidates—
  Tennessee—Biography.
Classification: LCC HV9955.T2 H38 2021 | DDC 364.8092 [B]—dc23
LC record available at https://lccn.loc.gov/2021013553

ISBNs: 978-1-5416-4630-8 (hardcover), 978-1-5416-4629-2 (ebook)

LSC-C

Printing 1, 2021

This book is dedicated to Shirlene "Pinky" German, my grandmother,
and Susie Lee "Sue Lee" German, my great-grandmother.
I miss you and love you always.

Nobody's free until everybody's free.

—FANNIE LOU HAMER

Contents

CONTENTS

"COUNT TIME!"
  "*Count Time!*"
"*On your feet!*"
"*Count Time!*"

Standing in my cinderblock cubicle next to my new roommate—or "bunkie," as I learned they were called—I watched the stone-faced corrections officers walk past each cubicle counting the women standing there. There was a cold glossiness in their eyes, so I didn't dare make eye contact.

One of the guards must have noticed that I was a new face because as he approached, he slowed up and stopped right in front of me.

"Name?" he asked.

"Keeda Haynes," I responded.

"Number?"

I looked down at the ID card hanging around my neck, remembering being told that we were required to wear it at all times so that we could be identified at any given moment. *Like cattle with cow tags, I* thought. *Or, like slaves.*

"00017. . . ." I read. ". . . 011."

The officer smirked as he walked away. "You'd better get used to that number; that's who you are now."

For the next almost four years, I was not Keeda J. Haynes, promising recent college graduate with aspirations of continuing on to law school. Instead, I was number 00017-011. An inmate, a statistic, a casualty of the War on Drugs in America, which had been ravaging Black and brown communities for decades.

All for a crime I did not commit.

Though the reality of the injustice was overwhelming, I refused to let this experience define me. I vowed that I would not let it be the end of my story.

My experiences as a Black woman in the criminal legal system have led me on a relentless journey to reimagine justice into a more equitable vision. My life's work, my personal mission, is devoted to dismantling the forces responsible for the fundamentally corrupt system our country is built on.

One of the pillars of our democracy is based on the idea of "equal justice under law." We've all heard this term in some form. The words are etched in stone on the US Supreme Court building in Washington, DC, derived, in part, from the Fourteenth Amendment to the US Constitution: "No State shall make or enforce any law which shall abridge the privileges or immunities of citizens of the United States; nor shall any State deprive any person of life, liberty, or property, without due process of law; nor deny to any person within its jurisdiction the equal protection of the laws."

But what does "equal justice under law" *really* mean? And is it actually equal for everyone?

For so many of us caught up in the criminal legal system, "equal justice under law" has been—and continues to be—an unfulfilled promise. Our current system of mass incarceration, at its very core, is deeply unjust and inhumane. It has relegated an astonishing number of people—overwhelmingly Black and brown—to a subclass of citizenry, deemed less deserving of dignity, respect, and equal protection under law. This system is beyond flawed—it has made a mockery of America's founding principles of democracy, opportunity, and basic human rights.

From the never-ending cycle of poverty and crime, to the injustice of mandatory minimum sentences and America's fictitious War on Drugs; from the damning power of prosecutorial discretion, tragic police-citizen encounters, and lack of accountability, to the difficulty of the formerly incarcerated transitioning back into their communities—the evidence pointing to the country's failures is overwhelming. It exposes a system that too often feels not like justice, but like "just us"—as in, those who don't have white skin.

In the United States there are over two million people behind bars—56 percent of whom are Black and brown. An additional five million Americans have already spent time in prison.

My story is just one of those millions.

GREW UP IN FRANKLIN, TENNESSEE, A SMALL, BLUE-COLLAR TOWN about twenty miles south of Nashville. Though time and the effects of gentrification have transformed the place into a more bustling hub in recent years, the Franklin of my childhood in the 1980s and 1990s was quiet, quaint, and familiar. Like many Southern cities, Franklin wore one version of its history proudly, while often ignoring other, messier versions that might dampen the mood during polite conversation. Traveling to Franklin's downtown, past old Victorian-style houses and shop windows filled with colorful candies, you're bound to run into Chip, a Confederate soldier forged in Italian marble, standing on a thirty-seven-foot-high pedestal in the middle of Franklin's public square. Gifted by the Daughters of the Confederacy in 1899, the inscription on the statue reads, in part: "In honor and memory of our heroes, both private and chief, of the Southern Confederacy. No country ever had truer sons, no cause nobler champions, no people bolder defenders than the brave soldiers to whose memory this stone is erected."

Franklin's place in Civil War history was considered a big deal. In 1864, a year before the Confederacy fell, the town was the site of a battle that ended in huge losses for the Confederate Army, ultimately turning the tide of the war against their favor. Thousands of soldiers—and many key generals and commanders—were injured or killed on Franklin soil. And so, in the years that followed, the entire town became a kind of memorial. My high school mascot was the Franklin Rebel, a cartoon of a smug Confederate soldier with a long handlebar mustache and matching beard. Every year we took school field trips to the Confederate cemetery and to all the Civil War sites across Franklin. I can't even count the number of times we visited the Carnton Mansion, a huge redbrick home sitting on forty-eight acres that was used as a field hospital during the Franklin battle. As schoolchildren we took these trips and learned the history lessons, yet we were never told that the historic mansion was built by the enslaved—that much of the town, in fact, was built by slave labor. Or that the war we were taught to memorialize was started to keep those who looked like me in chains. Or that after the war, when Jim Crow segregation became Southern law, Black and white people in our town began occupying separate parts of the city—parts where they have largely remained to this day.

There were some things you just didn't talk about—not with the white folks in town, and not with the Black folks, either. These were the stories behind the stories, ones you were never told and would likely miss if you weren't looking for them, and as a kid I was never looking for them; there was hardly reason to. Things were as they were—and as they had been for my mother, and her mother, and her mother before her. As it had been for all of my family who grew up in this town. Our own history in Franklin stretches back for generations—at least since the 1800s, depending on which part of the family you ask. We descend in part from the McLemores and the

Germans, whose plantations in Franklin are long gone, along with the pieces of our family history that have disappeared along with them. Such is the reality for many African Americans with roots in this country.

This is one level of truth. Layered on top of it is the Franklin I experienced during my childhood: a comfortable and ordinary place, filled with everybody I knew and loved. My maternal great-grandmother and grandmother, my parents and four siblings, and all my aunts, uncles, and cousins were born and raised here—nearly all of us living within a five- to ten-minute drive from one another. These people shaped the Franklin I understood; each of them was a star in the constellation of my life.

Most of the Black families in Franklin, including mine, occupied two or three pockets on the west side of town. Many of these families had lived in Franklin forever, and our lives and histories had become entwined over the years. Not only did everyone in Franklin know your name, they knew your mama's name, your daddy's name, and everyone else's name in your family. In the rare instance when someone might not, the elders could probably zigzag their way back to you through a long line of family friendships built from generations of being next-door, or down-the-block, or around-the-corner neighbors.

If my family was a constellation, it was my great-grandmother Sue Lee's home on Granbury Street that was the center of our little universe. Since Sue Lee moved into the neat white and grey home in 1938, it has been a sacred space for gatherings, meals, and fellowship, not just for our family but for the entire neighborhood. From her front porch that overlooked our block, Sue Lee would often sit in her favorite chair and greet folks as they came and went. It was not unusual for me as a kid to be sitting with her on a Sunday after church and hear car horns beeping, followed by people waving out of their car windows. It wouldn't be long before several of the grown-ups had parked on the sidewalk in front of the house and made their way to the porch to catch up with her or my grand-mother Pinky—or some combination of my aunts and uncles. I'd hop off the front steps and run around to the opposite end of the house to play with the other neighborhood kids who liked to gather in Sue Lee's backyard.

Pinky—Sue Lee's daughter, my mother's mother—lived about thirty minutes away in Nashville, but she was still as much a fix-ture in our world as everyone else. Always in and out of Sue Lee's house like the rest of us; she was there every Sunday before and after church, and for every church function, parade, or sports game that any one of us grandkids ever had.

My great-grandmother lived next door to another one of her daughters, my aunt Tit, and her husband Sammy James. And just a short drive from them was the home of my aunt Diane and her fam-ily, where I'd often go to pick vegetables from the garden. Corn, squash, turnip greens, green beans, peas—I spent more than one afternoon on Sue Lee's porch with my cousin Jamese, snapping beans gathered up from Diane's garden, doing whatever we were told to help prepare for that day's canning. Sue Lee's homemade cha-cha pickles were legendary, made with green tomatoes plucked straight from Diane's vines. Our neighbors would come around with their own jars of tomatoes for Sue Lee to make magic with. I often came into the house and found her bent over the little grinding machine she used to make the pickles, chopping and mixing and jarring for practically every family on the block. Whatever Diane didn't grow herself, the family would often buy from the Turnip Green Man, who came through the neighborhood on Saturdays, selling bushels of greens and watermelons and other produce from the back of his blue truck, where he also kept coolers of fresh fish he'd caught himself.

Every weekend, Sue Lee would wait on the porch in her chair for the Turnip Green Man to make his regular delivery.

Our neighborhood was interconnected by families as much as it was by streets. Next door to my aunt Tit and uncle Sammy James were the Lanes, with whom we shared the big grassy field behind our houses. The whole community used that field for cookouts and hangouts and neighborhood ball games. Across the street from the Lanes was Mr. Jim, who kept a fully stocked soda machine in his backyard, where everyone—kids and adults—would run between activities, or after church, or on scorching summer days to grab a cold drink. Then there was the snack bar at the other end of the field, owned by Mr. and Ms. Williams. You could go there and get a fried weenie sandwich with cheese and an ice cream and never—*never*—leave unsatisfied.

And amidst all this was my own immediate family: My mama and daddy, Stephanie and John; my older sister, Anitra; and my three younger brothers, Prince, then Tyke, and finally Johnathon. We never lived more than a ten-minute drive from Sue Lee's Granbury Street house growing up, and then when I was about in junior high, we eventually moved into a place on the same street. For each of my siblings and our cousins, the house, the street, the neighborhood and all its people were our entire world; the trails and land we traipsed through were our playground.

————

MY SIBLINGS AND I ARE ALL ABOUT TWO YEARS APART, SAVE FOR MY brother Johnathon, who came along seven years after Tyke was born. Tyke's first name is German, a family name on my mother's side, but since he was the baby of the family for so many years before Johnathon arrived, Tyke was always Tyke and the name just stuck, even after his position in the family changed. My sister, the eldest child, the studious one, actually goes by her middle name, Anitra. Her first name is Princess, which she never got around to using. "Anitra"—also known as "Pep"—just happened to catch on first. If the first girl in the family was Princess, it made sense, then, following my parents' logic, that the first boy would be called Prince. Born just after me, Prince, the class clown—always in trouble at school for cracking jokes and running his mouth—also goes by Count. This was a nickname my aunt Shawn, my mother's sister, gave him as a baby because of his pointy ears, which she always said reminded her of the Count on *Sesame Street*. Johnathon, the youngest, forever the kid brother in our lives, has always just been Johnathon to all of us.

And then there's me: Keeda Jarresse. Apparently my parents were convinced that I was going to be a boy when I was born—so when I wasn't, they were not prepared. They turned instead to the family for name suggestions, and it was my daddy's sister Peggy who offered up the winner. I was a small kid, the tiniest of my siblings, with just a little tuft of hair that sprouted on top of my head when I was a baby, so my uncle Steve took to calling me "Tweety Bird." Mama, not appreciative of her child being compared to a big-headed cartoon character, vetoed it immediately—but Steve still snuck in a "How you doing, Bird?" every once in a while. Daddy also liked to call me "Mo'Cheeks," because of my high cheekbones, but neither of these nicknames lasted like my siblings' did. And so, like Johnathon—who looks like my twin despite our ten-year age difference—I have always just been known by my given name, Keeda.

In fact, growing up, just being me was exactly the way I wanted it. I was fiercely independent, determined to go my own way regardless of what everyone else was doing. My mama loves to tell stories about how, as a baby, I would cry and cry because I only wanted to be around my sister. No one else would do, and I made this fact very known. When I approached the age when I should have been walking, my mama told me that I waited until I was good and ready to take that first step. I walked when I wanted to walk, not when everyone thought I was supposed to. As a kid stuck in the middle of a big family, I learned quickly that the best route to happiness was the one I could define for myself.

Though we moved around to a few different sections within Franklin's Black neighborhoods before settling on Granbury Street, in every home we had, Anitra and I shared a bedroom, and Prince and Tyke shared a room. With the four of us jostling for space, in and out of each other's rooms, eating, sleeping, and hanging out together, our household was always noisy—and even noisier after Johnathon was born. On any given day, it was filled with the loud banter of my brothers laughing, playing video games, or one kid yelling at another for wearing his or her clothes (usually me, trying to slip on Anitra's tops or jeans without her noticing). Weeknights were a regulated routine of homework, after-school sports practices, and nightly family dinners. Mama never let us miss our time spent together around the kitchen table.

On Saturday mornings, all four of us older siblings would get up early and eat our Cap'n Crunch or Frosted Flakes while watching cartoons. In the 1980s and 1990s, the superheroes you heard about most were guys: Superman, Spiderman, Batman, Robin. Of course, there was Wonder Woman and She-Ra too, but neither of them got as much attention. The truth was there were not many female superheroes out there, and when they did show up, they were often portrayed like Daisy Duke from *The Dukes of Hazzard*. Women in the public image were airheads like Daisy or damsels in distress—or like Betty Crocker, toiling away in the kitchen for their men. I was never the girl who played house and pined for an Easy Bake Oven—or deferred my strength or voice or shine to one of the boys. For those reasons alone, I *hated* most superhero shows and the fictitious worlds they portrayed. They were too limiting, too narrow, and left no room for my own imagination to kick into gear. I wanted, in every way, to be as unrestricted as possible. I was constantly chasing my freedom down—trying to figure out how to define it on my own terms.

One of my earliest memories exercising this particular personal drive happened in the second grade. It was Picture Day, and Mama had dressed me up for the occasion. She sent me off to Franklin Elementary wearing a frilly navy-blue and red dress with lace around the collar and wrists, complete with a matching quilted apron. My hair, normally in braids or a ponytail, was combed into two long spiral curled pigtails that made me look like the girly-girl I definitely was not. This was totally unacceptable. Come recess—a very serious time for me—I knew these clothes were not going to cut it on the playground, where I preferred to run free and wild. Determined not to be hampered, I secretly packed a T-shirt and shorts in my book bag that morning and headed out the door. As soon as my pictures were taken, I changed out of that dress and balled it up inside my bag, not even bothering to put it back on before heading home at the end of the day. When Mama saw me walk in wearing my muddy playclothes she was furious, thinking I had had my pictures taken that way.

I was a scrappy tomboy, never scared to play with my brothers during a neighborhood game of football, or let my allergies stop me from diving for a ground ball during a baseball game. (We kept a ready supply of Calamine lotion in our house to calm the hives that blossomed all over my body after days spent outside.) Despite the little bickering that may have occurred among my siblings behind closed doors, when we left the house Anitra, Prince, Tyke, and I—plus our cousins—moved as a united front. I may have been the smallest among us, but everyone knew that if you came for one of us, you'd have to get through me first. And we did everything together.

CHAPTER 1

Most weekends during our youth, if we were not riding bikes through the trails winding through our neighborhood or playing in the field behind Sue Lee's house, we were at Jim Warren Park for that day's games. My brothers played peewee football for the Williamson County Cowboys, the community league made up of Black and white kids throughout the town, and my cousins Jamese, Jana, Shawn, and I were cheerleaders for their team. When I got a little older, I started playing fast-pitch softball—one of the few sports outside of basketball (which I tried for one season, then never again) that girls in my town were allowed to play. I soon grew to love it—the speed, the skill it demanded, and the versatility it allowed me. I played outfield, shortstop, and pitcher, and mastered them all. I was one of only a handful of Black girls on my softball team, but I never felt the weight of that distinction while running the bases or striking out the players on our rival teams.

The Williamson County of my mother's childhood looked quite different, at least at a glance, from the one I grew up in. Hers existed in the time of Jim Crow, when the markers of where certain people could and could not go were clearly visible for everyone to see. Nearly everything in Franklin could be divided in Black and white: the water fountains and restrooms, the diners and parks, the streets where families built their lives. Downtown Franklin belonged to the white people; only on specific, predetermined occasions would you find yourself venturing there. When as a kid, Pinky took my mama and her sister Shawn for an ice cream at the Midway Café on Main Street, they knew to order their cones from the side door, and then to recede promptly to the other side of the divide, the same way they had come. Mama attended Natchez High, Franklin's only all-Black high school until Williamson County integrated its education system following the 1954 Brown v. Board of Education US Supreme Court decision, declaring segregated schools unconstitutional. It took Franklin seventeen years to implement the ruling, but in 1971, Natchez finally closed. The school, originally built in 1888, served as one of the few sources of education available to my ancestors and neighbors before me—including Pinky, a member of the graduating class of 1957. My mother was a freshman when the school closed, and she resented almost every day she spent at the mostly white Franklin High—a persistent reminder of all the experiences she and her fellow Black classmates had been denied.

By contrast, the integrated school system in Franklin was all I ever knew. Like most Black kids in town, I attended all the main public schools in the area, from elementary through high school. I was a part of integrated sports teams and played clarinet with a sea of white kids in the high school band. When my mother enrolled Anitra and me in Girl Scouts when I was about six and my sister was eight, we were the only Black girls in our respective troops. Every year when it came time for Girl Scout cookie season, we always cleaned up. Mostly because Mama, Aunt Shawn, and my grandmother Pinky loved a good competition. They were master saleswomen, racking up orders at church and from the factories where Mama and Shawn worked, or in Pinky's case, from Vanderbilt University, where she was a radiology technician. We had also cornered the market—we were the only Girl Scouts on our side of town. A few years later, when Anitra quit to pursue more teenage things, my cousin Jamese joined Troop 808 with me, followed soon after by my best friend Tangie. Then it was just the three of us—the brownest Brownies on our squad.

One of my closest friends in kindergarten was a white classmate named Anne Crane. Anne was even smaller than me and had long blonde hair she always pulled back into a ponytail. We shared a love for horses, and Anne's family had a horse farm in town. She'd often come to school telling me stories about what the horses had gotten up to the night before—the babies born or this or that funny thing that had happened between them while they were grazing in the pasture. The people I knew only kept cows, at the most, so this kind of fancy animal upgrade was exciting, and I was completely fascinated. Anne and I both collected "My Little Pony" dolls, and we loved to chase each other around the playground, galloping and neighing like we were one of them. But I never went to Anne's house to see the real horses she kept in her stables, and she never ventured to mine to see the collection of "My Little Ponies" I kept in the toy bin with my Barbies. Such playdates were never mentioned, and I think both of us knew, even at that age, not to ask for them.

"Racism," for me, was not a word I could even sniff in the air around me. There were no racial epithets hurled, nor people pointing me to "colored-only" ice cream shop entrances, as there had been during my mother and grandmother's times. Instead, it was embedded within that kind of inner knowing that happened with Anne, buried somewhere in my subconscious—a knowing you don't even know you know. But, of course, it was there all along—hidden underneath explanations like "Because that's just the way they've always been." Or, "This is how we've always talked about it." Or, "Our people have just always lived in these parts of town."

———

MARTIN LUTHER KING JR. ONCE OBSERVED THAT "ELEVEN O'CLOCK ON Sunday morning is one of the most segregated hours—if not the most segregated hour—in Christian America." While certainly some parts of Black and white Franklin had started coming together in the time since he first made this statement in 1960, MLK's words were pretty much as true then as they were when I was growing up—though I never would have seen things that way. Like the house on Granbury, church was just another place where the people most central to my world committed their time. My parents and siblings, my great-grandmother and grandmother, my aunt Diane, several of my cousins—practically the entire family—attended Providence United Primitive Baptist Church, located just down the road from Sue Lee's house, on the corner of Granbury and Natchez Streets. Built in 1883, the church had been a mainstay in Black Franklin for decades; many of the families who had lived alongside us in the neighborhood for generations also worshipped alongside us come Sunday.

My parents were so serious about our attendance at church that my siblings and I were not allowed to have or go to sleepovers on Saturday nights—ever. Missing church was simply not an option, so they removed any potential opportunity for excuses. Our before-church routine began, of course, at Sue Lee's house. We'd stop inside before taking the remaining two-minute walk to church, hoping she or my aunt Shawn had left breakfast out for us because they knew we were coming: Shawn's fried pork chops, if we were lucky, along with scratch-made biscuits and rice cooked with so much butter and sugar that it took on a yellowish tint and melted right in your mouth.

Entering through the red-carpeted vestibule for service, our family took our usual seats, always in the last benches from the back. From this vantage point, the entire scene of Providence on a Sunday morning was within our view. It was a small church, consisting of about fifty to a hundred members on a good day; each person playing a part to bring the energy of the place alive. Pinky and the other ushers led people to their seats—the cushions worn to the shape of the same congregants who filled them week after week. In a bank of benches on the left side of the sanctuary facing the choir, Sue Lee took her place beside the other Church Mothers. These elder matriarchs were some of the church's oldest living members; they held enough wisdom between them to fill an entire library. Opposite the Mothers sat the deacons, who began each service with a hymn and a prayer. These hymns are part of what makes Primitive Baptist churches what they are. They are not your traditional hymns; they weren't printed and bound in little books that we could reach for when the time came to sing. Our hymns were Negro spirituals, songs that were sung by our ancestors for hundreds of years, passed down from voice to voice, through our collective cultural memory alone. They had names like "Do Lord Show Me the Way" and "Before This Time Another Year"— ones that you might be hard-pressed to find in a Google search if ever you found yourself looking. As my daddy would say: "You'd have to catch the people who sang them to know them."

As soon as heads were raised after the deacons' prayer, the choir took their cue to march through the center aisle to the small riser behind the pulpit. Their songs accompanied each turn in the service: they followed the church announcements; they preceded Pastor Mosley's sermon and followed his closing prayer; they hummed underneath his invitation for new members to join; and they carried people out of their seats once the service was finally over.

Mama ensured that my siblings and I were at church practically as soon as the doors swung open for Sunday school at ten o'clock and for the regular service at eleven; for the afternoon service at three; and, more often than not, for the evening service too, which began at six thirty. Tuesday night youth choir rehearsal, Wednesday night Bible study, summers spent at Vacation Bible schools throughout the city—these experiences helped to form the shape, structure, and foundation of my life. Church was not just a place I attended, and faith was not just something I learned; they were interwoven within my family, tied up with my community, and surrounded every part of my childhood.

When I recall some of the things that bring me the most comfort, even now, I often think about the sights and sounds of Providence. I hear our piano player Amos Claybrooks singing "Grace and Mercy," his voice weaving a perfect cadence with the piano chords. I see

Glen Sowell with his eyes closed, taking his time with "I Stood on the Banks of Jordan," our entire congregation surrounding him with shouts of "Alright!" and "Go on now!" and "Amen!" If ever I were to hear the song "Joy," or "Every Day Is a Day of Thanksgiving," my mind would automatically dip back to our annual Choir Anniversary celebration, when several church choirs from around town would gather, singing songs made famous by big church groups like the Mississippi or Georgia Mass Choirs. My parents presided over the youth choir at Providence, in which all of us siblings (sometimes reluctantly!) participated. This meant that the Choir Anniversary was a major event in our household. The youth choir closed out the program every year, a chorus of fidgety boys and girls wearing matching cummerbunds and bow ties and dresses that Mama often spent all night making on her sewing machine.

Every February, the church held its Black History Month program. As was the case with the other seasonal performances we staged—at Easter and Christmas—every kid was given a speech to recite or a part to play. Standing in front of the pulpit, we were transformed into the Black history heroes we'd grown up with: mini George Washington Carvers and Sojourner Truths, retelling stories of African American achievement. When my sister got older, she wrote these plays herself, and Mama directed them. One year I was Harriet Tubman, leading escaped slaves to freedom through the Underground Railroad; another year I played a white lady who refused service to Black people at a 1960s lunch counter. And of course, no performance was complete without someone playing Martin Luther King Jr., which ended, always, with a recitation of "I Have a Dream." Afterward, we would all join hands as a church and sing "We Shall Overcome" and "Lift Every Voice and Sing."

These programs comprised all the elements of your typical Black history curriculum, both the figures and the music that soundtracked our most pivotal social movements as a people. "We Shall Overcome," "Lift Every Voice and Sing," I sang these songs year after year, learning the words without fully understanding their meaning, or how they may have been applied to Franklin's own racial history. To me, back then, they were just a few of our many church traditions—conjured up with the same fond memories I have of caroling at hospitals and nursing homes with the choir at Christmastime or of Easter Egg hunts on the church lawn. These experiences, where I was surrounded by my entire family, taught me that faith was inextricable from the community it was formed around; that religion in practice was an act of family, a demonstration of love.

———

THIS IS THE POINT WHEN I SHOULD PROBABLY MENTION THAT DESPITE the absolute, genuine joy I felt being around my family and community, I reveled in my alone time too. I was, and will always be, a bit of an introvert. With four siblings, two parents, grandparents, great-grandparents, cousins, aunts, uncles, neighbors, and church people constantly revolving around me, I often felt drained by so much interaction. Some of the activities I liked most during these years were the ones I could do alone, and there was no greater escape for me than the one I could find in the pages of a good book. We didn't have any bookstores in town at the time, so I was often holed up at the Franklin Public Library or parked in front of our local Boys and Girls Club's bookshelves, where I spent many afternoons after school. The arrival of the Scholastic Book Fair catalog was one of my favorite times during the school year—I couldn't wait to take it home and try to convince Mama to buy me every single book in the catalog (of course she refused, but I still always managed to snag a few).

I read *everything*: mysteries and suspense novels and newspaper comics—anything that could quiet the day-to-day noise around me, and, especially as I got older, that could transport me to a world beyond the one I knew so well. I spent my entire upbringing surrounded by familiarity: I knew every contour of my neighborhood, the rhythms of Franklin's routines, the same string of faces in my community year in and year out. But when I was reading, my imagination could take me anywhere; I could put myself in the shoes of anyone, and try on different versions of who I might eventually want to become.

Entering my teenage years, I didn't know exactly what I wanted to be when I grew up, but I started to carry with me a feeling that my imagination just might be bigger than Franklin could contain. There is safety in security and deep love in the familiar, for sure. But somewhere during my transition from Keeda the tomboy kid to Keeda the introspective teen, those sources of comfort began to rub up against an even bigger need. I began to realize that I wanted more than the stories that so often played out in my town: of the high school romances that turned into marriages; of having the 2.5 kids and the house with the white picket fence in the same neighborhood where you grew up; of the graduations from the same schools and the promotions at the same jobs that everyone in Franklin neatly slotted into. There had to be something different out there from what I'd always known, this place where everybody—and I do mean *everybody*—knew your name and your business, whether you wanted them to or not.

I started thinking about what it would feel like to walk into a crowd somewhere like New York City, where no one knew who I was. No one asking me if I was Stephanie's daughter or Pinky's granddaughter; no one tracing my family roots through the blocks we've always lived on. A place like New York City was big enough to fit whatever hopes and dreams you could put into it; big enough that people could exist in a world created entirely by their own design, instead of the one they'd been born into. Franklin was where I was from, and I was proud of that. It was the town that supplied all the people and memories I loved. But by sixteen—and probably even in the years before—I began to doubt whether it was the place I truly belonged.

I craved new stories, not the old ones that had been written and rewritten a million times. To get to them, something told me I needed to experience what was outside of the world that had raised me. And so I moved through my daily high school routines with an eye toward a future beyond Franklin. One I couldn't name just yet, but I knew was out there—somewhere—for me to grab hold of. Until then I returned, again and again, to the universes held inside the pages of my books. I read to think bigger and to feel deeper, and to explore as far as my mind could take me.

When I was in the twelfth grade, I remember being assigned Night, by Elie Wiesel. It's a small book, barely a hundred pages, but it's packed with so much information and emotion. Wiesel was a Holocaust survivor, and Night tells the story of his experiences in a concentration camp as a teenager. It was my first real introduction to the Holocaust, and while the book is filled with vivid descriptions of its horrors, what shook me most was the sheer strength of Wiesel's will. Here was someone who had been through more at sixteen than most of us experience in our whole lifetimes, and still, he had come out on the other side. Scarred, absolutely, but not broken. I can remember staying up late in my room, reading and rereading passages where he talks about fighting against becoming a victim of his circumstances. He would not let the horribly oppressive system the Holocaust produced strip him of his humanity. He refused to become what they tried to turn him into.

As a seventeen-year-old Black girl from a small town in Tennessee with zero experiences that even came close to what Wiesel endured,

I couldn't say why this particular message resonated so deeply with me. Though, of course, now it's clear. At the time, I just knew that this man and his determination moved me. His words would stick close to my spirit, echoing in a way I never could have imagined in the years to come.

chapter 2

LIFE IN FRANKLIN AFTER HIGH SCHOOL LARGELY FLOWED IN ONE OF
two directions: either work a blue-collar job at one of the factories in town—making fans at Lasko, water heater parts at Apcom, or
whatever else the town produced at the various other manufacturers
in town—or go to college nearby. Tennessee State University, thirty-
five minutes away in Nashville; Middle Tennessee State University,
about an hour east in Murfreesboro; Tennessee Tech, a little further
out in Cookeville; Columbia State Community College—these were
your options. While much of my family had worked in the factories
at different points in their lives, I knew that to start building the life
I wanted, college was my only path.

There were no high school counselors available at school to help
us plan for our futures based on what excited us most, at least no
one who particularly stands out to me now. "Dreaming big" was
not something Franklin public schools necessarily advocated; even
contemplating college out of state was rarely brought up. But even
without that kind of guidance, I took my own interests seriously. For
as long as I could remember, I had always been drawn to the "why"

of things. What goes into making a person? How do our experiences, our circumstances, shape who we become? What makes people do what they do? I remember watching the movie *The Silence of the Lambs* for the first time and being fascinated by Jodie Foster's character. Clarice Starling, promising Quantico trainee, is plucked from her position in the Behavioral Science Unit of the FBI to interview incarcerated serial killer Hannibal Lecter. She's tasked with trying to get to the bottom of *why* he was so compelled to murder. Lecter's insights, they hoped, might help the authorities catch another serial killer on the loose, and prevent similar crimes from happening in the future.

Watching that film—seeing Jodie Foster try to get to know Hannibal Lecter, understand his actions, and apply that understanding to finding a solution—I thought: *If you can figure out why people do what they do, then you can solve the problem.* I felt certain that there was something powerful about understanding and about being understood, especially when it came to problem-solving—another concept that had always captured my attention. If you understand *why* something is happening—why serial killers kill, why burglars commit burglaries, why abusers abuse—then, it seemed to me, you'd have the best possible shot at fixing it. It didn't make sense to solve a problem without knowing all the factors that might be contributing to it. Talking to people who'd done things society had deemed wrong, figuring out what makes them tick and how to help them and our communities—this was something I deeply wanted to do. It was the ultimate problem-solving exercise, and the stakes couldn't be higher.

And so, when I graduated from Franklin High School in the spring of 1996, I set my sights on becoming a criminal psychologist. With no car of my own yet and no desire to live in the dorms with strangers (Anitra had left for college two years before, and I finally—*finally*—had a room all to myself), that fall I started taking classes at Columbia State Community College right in town and continued to live at home with my parents and brothers. During this time, my interest in all things criminal psychology deepened by the day. I pored over true crime books, especially ones about well-known serial killers. I got my hands on as many of these stories as I could find. I wanted to work with serial killers most, I discovered, partly because no one else wanted to. Their outcast status told me that these individuals were probably the most misunderstood and therefore the most in need.

I remember going to a bookstore in Nashville one day and buying an encyclopedia on serial killers. I read all the books I could find on John Wayne Gacy, Ted Bundy, and the Gainesville Ripper—a guy named Danny Rolling who had murdered several students at the University of Florida in 1990. Many of these books didn't just provide the gory details of the serial killers' crimes, they also explored the environments that made them—their childhoods, their parents, their relationships, the big experiences that shaped them. These kinds of insights, I learned, formed crucial lines in the total blueprint of a person's life. By paying attention to these things, I could better understand the person they eventually became.

Armed with these developing interests and an urgency to keep pushing myself to learn more, after a year at Columbia State, I decided to transfer to Tennessee State University (TSU) in Nashville, where Anitra was about to enter her junior year.

It was at this juncture in my life, at the start of so many new beginnings, that I met C.

I had just turned nineteen in July of 1997. It was the summer before my first fall semester at TSU, and Anitra and I went out to a club in Nashville to celebrate her twenty-first birthday. At the end of a fun and uneventful night, the two of us and a few of our friends exited the Music City Mix Factory downtown and were waiting to cross the street to get to our car. The road in front of the Mix Factory was packed with people spilling out from all the clubs nearby. They came from every direction, weaving between the slow-moving cars that were also trying to make their way through the crowds.

Seeing us waiting to cross the street from inside his own car, C paused to let us pass, and as we did, he called out to me to come over to his open window. We exchanged hellos and how are yous, and as much information as we needed to know that we were both interested in talking more.

"C," I learned, was the nickname he often went by, his full name was Myron Seymore Armstrong. He was cute: clean-cut, light-brown skin, light eyes, a little older than me—twenty-four, he said. He told me he lived in Memphis, where he had grown up, but was staying in Nashville for the summer for an internship he was doing. Plus, he added, he was doing some work in town for the pager and cell phone business he had started with his cousins—"Beepers Plus," they called it. I decided that I liked his vibe; C was different from the guys in Franklin I was used to, more put-together maybe, and I didn't hesitate to give him my number that night when he asked.

We talked a few more times throughout that summer—surface level, getting-to-know-you conversations that now blend in with so many other activities happening in a typical, busy nineteen-year-old's life: working, staying out too late, going out too much with my friends, and preparing for the start of a new year at a new school. We continued to chat a bit once my fall semester at TSU began, but by that October the communication between us had fizzled; C stopped calling, and I got too swept up in the pace of my day-to-day to really care.

I entered TSU as a psychology major, and my days were a constant balancing act of gen-eds and psych classes and statistics requirements, and working retail full-time at Cool Springs Galleria, a mall in nearby Cool Springs, where I'd had different clothing store jobs since high school. I organized my class schedule around my commutes back to Franklin, switching between my role as student and the co-manager position I held at the Body Shop.

Opting out of the workforce was never an option for my siblings and me. I got my first job at fifteen, bagging groceries at the local Kroger to earn my spending money. All of us had to work—our parents didn't pay for much; they couldn't even if they wanted to. Both of them worked various jobs to pay the bills—*their* bills—which meant that once my brothers, sister, and I were old enough, we each had to do the same. To be able to put gas in our cars, we had to work. To buy clothes, food while we were out—anything we wanted—we had to work. When I got to college, I paid for tuition with loans I took out myself. I paid for my own school books and supplies. I got my first car—a used forest-green Dodge Neon—with a refund check from my student loans. Anything my siblings and I had, we had to get on our own, however we were going to get it. This meant there was little time left for the typical college life.

TSU provided a completely different environment from Columbia State. I went from attending classes at a quiet, zero-activity community college to being immersed in a bustling, lively HBCU (historically Black college or university). There were people everywhere—traveling in groups from class to class; migrating from the student center or cafeteria to gather in the big courtyard between the two buildings, where DJs spun music on certain days—the fraternities and sororities on full display, especially during Greek week. I hung out at school whenever I could—definitely during homecoming and after class if I had time to kill before work—but a lot of the campus activities remained in the background for me because work ate up so much of my schedule.

The cycle of my life continued this way: school, work, school, work, school, work, school, work—broken up occasionally by nights out with friends, whenever I wasn't completely tied up with my other two commitments. And then, in early 1999—a full year and a half after I last heard from him—C called me out of the blue. "Hey, we met at the Mix Factory. This is C," he said when I answered the phone.

"C?" I replied after a minute. "Oh yeah, I remember you."

———

DURING THAT PHONE CALL, C EXPLAINED THAT HE WAS HOPING WE could pick back up again where we left off. "I was wondering if you'd still be single," he said to me. I thought I could hear him smiling over the phone. I was surprised—and pretty flattered, really. That kind of undivided attention from someone you're interested in is alluring at any age, but especially for a now twenty-year-old whose relationship experience up to that point had amounted to only a couple of dates here and there. Nothing exciting to report. But then, here comes this guy—nice, older, with his shit all-the-way together, it seemed—who was popping back into my life with the specific intention of pursuing me, when he could have pursued anyone. It wasn't long before I fell for him.

With C a little over three hours away in Memphis, the telephone became our lifeline. Talking before classes and after work, during lunch breaks and commutes, while getting ready first thing in the morning and settling down for bed at night, the connection between us grew. We were both from big, tight-knit families—he only had one sibling, a sister, but his cousins were like brothers to him. He was a preacher's kid; he didn't go to church like I did, but he knew what it was like to grow up with it closely tied to your everyday life. He had a young son who lived with his mother in California but who visited C and his parents during most summers.

CHAPTER 2

He liked the ambition in me; we talked a lot about my goals, my desire to become a criminal psychologist, and the way I supported my education by juggling my full course load with my job at the Body Shop. C, for his part, was ambitious too—working at a bank in Memphis along with working at the beepers and pagers business he'd mentioned starting with a few of his cousins when we met that first summer in 1997. In the time since we last spoke, they'd opened another store location. C and his cousins now had a Beepers Plus kiosk inside a mall in Memphis, he told me, in addition to a brick-and-mortar shop in Nashville, over on Murfreesboro Road.

The facts of our lives seemed to add up nicely together. But just like the Franklin I personally experienced versus the more complicated one that was never discussed, here, again, we have only one level of truth. Layered on top of this one is what I would come to find out only years later. That when C and I first met outside the Music City Mix Factory in Nashville during the summer of 1997, he was in town for business. But that business, at least in part, was selling marijuana. Beepers Plus, as C had mentioned, was in fact a family-run enterprise—but the full picture was that it was an enterprise that allowed the cousins to funnel drugs from California, where C's cousin Travis lived, to Tennessee, where they would then distribute them between Memphis and Nashville. And when the calls between C and me fizzled out that October, and I didn't hear from him again for over a year, it was, in part, because our lives got busy. But what I did not know was that during that same month in October, C had been arrested in a police raid at the house of a dealer they were working with. He spent a couple of days in jail and was eventually sentenced to probation. Things settled down for a while, and then C and his cousins began discussions about starting up the operation again. This time, they set Nashville as the center of their activities.

It was with this crucial layer of truth hidden from my view that C picked up the phone and called me again.

———

ALMOST IMMEDIATELY AFTER C AND I RECONNECTED IN EARLY 1999, WE were speaking every day, long-distance. Communication was easy with him—the more we spoke, the more integrated into everyday life our talks became. "Hearing your voice gets me started for the day," he would say when he reached out to me soon after he woke up in the morning. He called on his way to work at the bank and in spare moments during the day; he called on his drive home and later on in the evening too, while he played video games in the house he shared with his cousins Larry and Marcus. We spoke while I did homework, and long after the rest of my family went to sleep for the night. C and I talked so much that, honestly, the content of much of these early conversations is now lost to me. It seemed like we spoke about every single little thing and about nothing at all.

And so, it didn't seem unusual when, about a month after we fell back into each other's lives, C casually asked if a few of his Beepers Plus packages could be sent to me directly, since FedEx's delivery schedule didn't match up with his and his cousins' store hours, and the cousins were afraid of their pager and cell phone shipments getting stolen. He said this had happened a few times when boxes were left outside the door. "You'd be doing me a big favor," C told me one day over the phone. The process he outlined was simple: he'd have the packages delivered to me at home or down the street at Sue Lee's—where I also got mail sent sometimes—and then one of the cousins would drop by later that day to pick them up. Usually his cousin Nate but sometimes Larry too. (They both had more flexible schedules during the day than C did, he explained.) Knowing that, as a college student, I could always use the cash, C even offered to throw me $50 per delivery for my trouble. It seemed like a good deal to me—receive a few packages and collect a few extra bills along the way. I agreed to help him out, not giving much thought to the details.

Of course, looking back, I could not have known just how much this favor would eventually cost me. That, in accepting those packages, I had actually agreed to be the recipient of boxes filled with drugs—completely without my knowledge. The shipments that I assumed carried cell phones and pagers, as I was led by C to believe, actually contained bricks of marijuana for the cousins' illegal operation.

Once or twice a week, a FedEx person walked up to the porch of our house on Granbury Street and set down the boxes just outside the door, where they would remain—untouched and unopened by me—until Larry or Nate drove up from Memphis to retrieve them. When they arrived, we would catch up for a bit—Nate, especially, *loved* to talk—then they'd be on their way. Month after month things progressed this way: chatting with C on the phone throughout my day, rushing around between school in Nashville and work near Franklin, and occasionally being around to scribble my signature on a FedEx receipt whenever one of their boxes arrived. The deliveries became an afterthought in the normal course of my routine, something I passed on my way out or in but otherwise paid little attention to.

That April, I started a new job as an assistant manager at another clothing store called Wet Seal, which meant that I would be dividing my time between the store's two locations: one inside the same mall I'd been working at in Cool Springs and the other at Hickory Hollow Mall, which was a little further out in a suburb of Nashville. Between these new work obligations and my class schedule at TSU, I told C that I would rarely be at home to accept the packages. But he was accommodating, catering to my needs, trying to make things as easy for me as possible. He suggested that they could send the packages to my job instead, at whichever location I'd be that day. "We could even try to have them delivered at the same time as your regular store shipments," he offered one afternoon. "Then Nate or Larry can just pick them up from there." What I took at the time to be a thoughtful gesture, I know now was a good opportunity for C and his cousins. Having more addresses at their disposal to send the drug packages to meant more diversity in their pickup locations. More diversity in their pickup locations made detecting patterns in these deliveries a little less obvious to someone, at any point down the line, who might be looking. And so, with that disguised logic at play, C's packages also started being mailed to me at work, often delivered by FedEx along with the boxes of new clothing stock I received and processed regularly at Wet Seal.

Whenever FedEx brought a shipment in, I just moved the big, rectangular boxes I knew to be inventory to the back of the store and left C's boxes exactly where the delivery guys had dropped them. I knew the Beepers Plus boxes by sight at this point—they were smaller and squarer than the ones we received for the store—which made them easy for me to ignore, and I'd carry on with my work. A lot of times I'd be at the back counter, busy cross-checking the shipment or unpacking clothes or doing markdowns, when I'd look up from my tasks to see that Larry or Nate had appeared—waving to me from the front of the store. Just like when they came by the house, we would catch up for a little while if I wasn't tied up with a customer, then they'd scoop up their boxes and be on their way.

During that same month of April 1999, C and I saw each other, face-to-face, for the first time since we reconnected earlier in the year. We hadn't been together in-person since that very first time we met outside the Mix Factory two summers before. DMX was having a concert at TSU, and C came up for the show. Up until this point, our new relationship had deepened from a distance, sustained and nurtured by those frequent calls that brought us closer with each conversation. After our reunion, we quickly made plans to get together again, this time in Memphis the next month for the city's annual Memphis in May festival.

Piling into my forest-green Neon, I set out on the three-hour drive west with two of my best friends, Eden and Christana. I'd met Christana in high school when we both first started working at the mall in Cool Springs. She was a sales associate at a clothing store called Rave, and I was working across the corridor from her at Deb, a similar store that also specialized in clothing geared toward teens. During breaks, Christana would come into my store to look around, browsing through the racks, and I would do the same at hers. We were both among the few Black people working at our respective stores, so it was hard for us to miss each other. One night after work, I saw that she was waiting for a ride, and since my dad was already on his way to pick me up, I offered to take her home. She lived in Brentwood, a town about twenty minutes north of Franklin, in the same county. After that night, we became fast friends, talking all the time, bonding over fashion and clothes.

Christana met Eden a few years later in college—they both went to Middle Tennessee State University (MTSU). They were also both from Nigerian families who found themselves living in the South. Eden lived in Hermitage, another small town on the outskirts of Nashville. It was through their connection that Eden and I became close as well. Christana was the most reserved among us, and I was a little less so—I still had an introverted side, but I liked to go out every once in a while. But Eden was the funny, goofy, life of the party—and she was *always* looking for one. Collectively, the three of us balanced each other out. Eden, Christana, and I were a dynamic trio. Almost everything we did, we did together.

Arriving in Memphis for the first of several trips we would take together to visit C, we stayed in the house he shared with Larry and

Marcus. From there, it was not far to Beale Street, where much of the Memphis in May festivities always took place. The entire month was an explosion of activity: outdoor concerts along the Mississippi River; a huge barbecue competition in the center of the city; and a constant flow of people hopping from bar to bar, venue to venue, throughout Memphis's downtown. This was C's stomping ground, he grew up in Memphis, and it was amazing to experience just how different the environments that raised us were. Winding our way through Beale Street, we saw everybody there, together: Black folks and white folks too—everyone being as loud and boisterous as they wanted to be.

Memphis had its own history of racism, of course: MLK was assassinated in 1968 on the balcony of the city's Lorraine Motel, leading to weeks of protests in town and all over the country. Almost eighty years before that, in 1892, a white mob burned down the printing office of journalist Ida B. Wells's Memphis newspaper, *The Free Speech*, angry that she had refused to stop reporting on the recent lynchings in town. And in more recent years, turmoil over police violence, political power, and everyday racism against Black people had bubbled up periodically for decades.

But Memphis had also long been an epicenter of Blackness. It was one of the largest cities in Tennessee, and *we* made up the majority. Memphis birthed American blues and influenced Southern soul music. It was a major site of activism during the civil rights movement of the 1950s and 1960s. And Beale Street, where we found ourselves most often during that Memphis in May festival weekend—jostling shoulder-to-shoulder with strangers as we moved together with the crowds—was at the center of it all. Beale Street was once home to the city's concentration of Black-owned businesses, restaurants, and clubs. It was where musicians like B. B. King and Muddy Waters and Louis Armstrong often performed. Though the street, and the city itself, had undergone some economic and demographic shifts in the years since, the essence of the same *we-are-here* energy remained.

That kind of relatively unbothered, unchecked freedom that Memphis embodied, specifically when it came to Black people, was a new experience for Christana, Eden, and me. In the places where we were from, Black people and white people had their place. In the places we were from, the police always found a way to show up wherever Black people gathered, for no other reason than to remind us they were there. To send the message that we may be living in these neighborhoods, but they were the ones controlling them. I started noticing this especially in Franklin during high school in the early 1990s, which, coincidentally or not, overlapped with a huge uptick in the town's population. Between 1990 and 2000, Franklin more than doubled in size—from just over 20,000 to nearly 42,000. The explosion in numbers was largely in response to Nashville's rapid growth, which drove (mostly white) people to nearby suburbs, like Franklin. During this time, I noticed the local police creeping in from the periphery. Suddenly, they were everywhere: constantly riding through our neighborhood, slowly circling the block near Natchez and Granbury in their cars or bikes—sometimes even walking the blocks on foot. "Patrolling the area," they would call it. But they never patrolled white areas the way they did ours.

Memphis, by contrast, was a completely different story—and Memphis in May brought this contrast out in full view. Gathered by the hundreds, here Black folks were walking and talking and acting freely, without the police policing them just for existing. *This is freedom*, I thought. Eden, Christana, and I loved going to Memphis—and I loved that C was in Memphis too. It was the closest thing to disappearing into those New York City–like crowds that I'd experienced in my life so far.

chapter 3

ON THE CAR RIDE HOME FROM MEMPHIS, OUR BANK ACCOUNTS depleted after a weekend spent enjoying the city, Christana, Eden, and I laughed and joked about how broke we all were. It was a typical topic of conversation—such is life in your early twenties, I think, for a lot of us anyway: the lifestyle you want outpaces the financials you actually need to get there. Keeping your nose to the grindstone while you build the scaffolding of your future, this was the reality for me and my friends at the time.

Eden, though, had a few additional things to navigate on top of this: she'd recently had a baby, and as a result, she was forced to press pause on school and work. She and her daughter were currently living at home in Hermitage with Eden's mom, whom Eden had never gotten along with—the two of them were constantly butting heads. While we were away that weekend, baby Imani stayed at our house on Granbury, where she was often looked after by the village of my family—my mom, my sister, Pinky or Sue Lee or one of the aunts—whenever Eden happened to need a babysitter.

Talking as much as we did, C was familiar with the different stories that surrounded my life—including those of my friends—and knew all about Eden's situation. When it happened to come up in conversation one night while we were all in Memphis, C thought of an idea: "What if Eden accepted some packages?" The question was framed as an offering, a piece of generosity he could extend to my friend, knowing that money was tight and her flexibility was limited because of the baby. It seemed to me like an easy way Eden could pocket a few dollars while she was figuring out her next steps.

Shortly after we returned from the trip, C's idea came up again. Eden told me she was interested and asked what she would have to do. I explained that she would just need to be around to accept the Beepers Plus packages at her house, then Larry or Nate would come by later that day to pick them up. Eden gave me her address to give to C—which I promptly lost amid the million other things I was wrapped up in between work and the end of my spring semester at school. I managed to successfully pass it along when she gave it to me a second time, and within a couple of weeks, C had coordinated with Eden to send her the first package.

The morning the box was scheduled for delivery, I was woken up early by the sound of my phone ringing. "Keeda, get up." It was C. "Why?" I responded, confused by the tone of his voice. "Because Eden is not at home." Apparently, he told me, when Nate called over to Eden's house to see whether the package had come, her mom answered the phone and said she wasn't there. "Well, what do you want me to do about it?" I asked, still confused. One, I was never really involved in the scheduling of anyone's deliveries, so bringing this to me in the first place was strange. And two, none of what I was hearing sounded serious enough to warrant disrupting my sleep. If Eden wasn't home at that exact moment, she would be soon enough, I figured. "Well, call her house and see if she's there now," C said, insistent.

This, in hindsight, should have been my first red flag.

I hung up the phone with C and called Eden myself, like he asked. This time, she answered. She said she just got home—she'd stepped out for a bit to visit a friend who lived in the apartment across the hall. "But my mom opened the box," she added, clearly annoyed. Eden described the mess in her living room—there was duct tape and plastic, foam packaging peanuts and bits of torn cardboard absolutely everywhere. She had walked through the door to her mom screaming and yelling at her—obviously angry, but about what exactly, Eden wasn't sure. "Now she's locked herself in the bathroom with the package. Overreacting, like typical Grace." Eden gave me more play-by-plays of what was happening, the arguing going on between her and her mom. "She's saying there's marijuana in there, and she's going to call the police."

What? The whole scene was not quite computing. Eden's mom was known for her hysterics, as Eden characterized it, and the way Eden was talking about the situation made it seem like whatever was happening over there was more of the same. She seemed to be more irritated with her mom's behavior than anything else. But still—I'd also heard the words "package" and "marijuana" and "police." Did her mom find weed in the box with the beepers and cell phones? Did she find a joint? A little baggy? I had no idea and neither did Eden, since the package was locked away in another room before she could see what was inside.

I called C back to tell him what I'd heard. When I got to the part about the marijuana, he was seemingly just as shocked and confused as I genuinely was. His response made it seem like we were both caught off guard. In reality, this was a potential disaster for him and his cousins. Not only were they at risk of losing their supply for the day—the packages delivered to Eden's place contained way more than a joint's worth of weed—they were also at risk of their cover story being blown. Eden and I would later find out that the boxes they *said* were filled with cell phones and pagers actually contained nothing remotely close to those things. And if anyone got arrested, that might really put a wrinkle in their plans. Behind the scenes, away from Eden and me, the cousins immediately switched to damage control. Once Travis was looped in—the cousin responsible for sending the drugs from California, where he lived—he bounced between calls with C and Nate, telling them to find some way of getting that package out of Eden's house.

"Do you think she'll actually call the police?" C asked me, referring to Eden's mom. He wondered if it might be a good idea for me to go over to Eden's myself to get a better sense of what was going on. When I told him that I wasn't driving forty minutes to Hermitage, he had us call Eden back together, on a three-way call. He wanted to know if Eden could somehow get the package back from her mom and leave it outside for Nate, who was now on his way. C didn't know a thing about any marijuana, he said again; he just didn't want to lose the money they'd spent on those phones and pagers. He was adamant about getting what was theirs back from Eden's mom. But when we talked to Eden again a few minutes later, she said that it was too late: her mom was refusing to let the package go, and she had already called the police. "I cannot believe she's acting like this," Eden said at one point, commotion filling the background.

We kept getting disconnected. I called, Nate called, C and I called together, but each time we tried to reach Eden to see what was happening, her mom got on the line and told us to stop calling her house, then hung up the phone. It was confusion, heaped upon chaos on all sides. Nate showed up at Eden's apartment before the police did, hoping that he might still be able to get the package out before they arrived. But the cops knocked on the door soon after he got there and arrested him and Eden both.

CHAPTER 3

Later that night, Eden phoned me from jail to say that they would be releasing her, and I called Christana so the two of us could pick her up. They never told Eden what she was being charged with, and she still, at that point, didn't know how much marijuana was found in the box—neither of us did. Whatever it was couldn't have been that serious, I reasoned at the time, because she was let go without even having to post bail.

When Eden climbed into the car at the police station, she was fuming. "What kind of mother calls the cops on her own daughter?!" All of the day's anger, intensity, and disbelief was bottled up and pointed directly at her mom. There was no way I was going to take Eden home with emotions still running that high, so I drove her and Christana back to my house on Granbury instead. Sitting in my living room, we tried to make sense of the last few hours, the shock hanging over us all. At some point during all the back-and-forth phone calls, Nate had told Eden that he had no idea what was going on, or how the weed had gotten there—the same story C had told me. The narrative they painted made it seem like we were *all* in the dark. No one—not C or Nate, not Eden or me—seemed to know what the hell had just happened.

In the coming days, C and his cousins got to work aligning their stories, rebuilding the façade. Under the guise of getting to the bottom of it himself, C reported back to say that Travis admitted that he knew about the marijuana in Eden's package—he'd put it there. And that Nate, even though he'd initially told Eden otherwise, knew about it too. It was a one-time thing that they were trying out on their own—just during that *one* delivery to Eden—to see if they could pull it off. "I guess they were trying to make a little extra money on the side," C explained. They did it entirely behind C's back, he told me, without his knowledge. "Travis and them know that they could never try that with you," he told me. The boxes I received during the last few months, he said, had always only ever contained beepers and cell phones. "They know how much you mean to me—they know what you're in school for. And they know if they messed that up for you, they would have to answer to me."

The reassurances in the weeks after the Eden Incident kept on coming. C didn't miss an opportunity to tell me how much Travis and Nate had messed up; how sorry he was about Eden; how Travis kept reassuring him that it had never happened before. I went down to Memphis at least a couple of times right afterward, so that C could tell me all of this again, to my face. Eden came along with me on one occasion too. Over and over and over, he claimed his ignorance and apologized for his cousins going rogue.

But I was still wary, and C knew it. He doubled down on the explanations, even arranging for me to talk to Travis myself over the phone one day—something I rarely did. "Keeda, listen: we've never sent you *any* marijuana, we would never, ever do that to you. C would kill us if we tried." He was just as adamant as C had been. "I'm so sorry, it was just the one time. Nate and I were just trying to get some extra money. I swear, C didn't even know." Each of the cousins kept reinforcing their mutually agreed-upon version of the truth. They had their stories down pat. What happened with Eden was an unfortunate slipup, done completely behind C's back. It was a mistake, a blip in their otherwise "legitimate" business venture.

A business venture that still needed to stay active, as C reminded me once things calmed down. I assumed, of course, that he meant Beepers Plus, selling beepers and cell phones. But in reality, despite the recent scare, the cousins were eager to resume their drug operations. "We've gotta keep our business going, Keeda," C mentioned one day, carefully broaching the topic of me accepting packages again. "I promise you—I *promise you*—I would never do anything to jeopardize your future."

chapter 4

THREE WEEKS AFTER EDEN AND NATE WERE ARRESTED, I RESUMED accepting the packages at home and at work, convinced that C was telling the truth. Convinced too, through the cousins' united front of a story, that what happened with Eden must have been a fluke—a horrible situation but ultimately an anomaly. I never saw Nate picking up the packages again, which further reassured me that they had removed him as the bad apple and just wanted to carry on with their normal course of business. (In truth, because he was arrested, he had a target on his back, so they had to take him out of the rotation.) From that point forward, I only saw Larry for the pick-ups or sometimes their other cousin Marcus. Plus, nothing further happened to Eden after she was let off jail. No court appearances, no fines, no probation. Proof, she and I both thought, that Eden's mom must have been overreacting about what she saw in that box. Everything had been blown way out of proportion, but now it was settling back into place.

Throughout all of this, school and work continued to be the two primary modes I operated on, outside of C. Even though I had just successfully completed my first year at TSU, the idea of doing another while still living at home was daunting. I needed to get out from under my parents' roof and try living on my own. I wanted to work more hours to make more money at the mall, but I also needed more time in the day to fit everything I was trying to cram in. What I needed, when it really came down to it, was a different way of pursuing the things I was after: independence and a job that both paid the bills and aligned with the criminal psychology career I still wanted for myself.

I spent the summer of 1999 figuring things out, and by that August, with a new job search behind me, I had a plan. I wrote to TSU to give notice that I would be taking some time off school. And then I got back to the Davidson County Sheriff's Department in Nashville, gladly accepting their job offer.

By September of 1999, I was officially on the county's payroll, writing parking tickets as a meter maid.

When I accepted the position in the County Sheriff's Department, five other new recruits and I were given two options: either complete academy training and go straight into the jails to work as a correctional officer (CO)—my ultimate goal—or go through the Public Works Department first, working in the Parking Division for a little while, then transition into the jails. The pay would be the same, but the hours were much more reliable, writing parking tickets. It would be a regular, Monday through Friday, forty-hour per week job, without the extra burden of potentially having to work weekends and holidays. Coming straight out of my retail schedule at the mall in Cool Springs—where I often had to give up my evenings, along with my Saturdays and Sundays—this proposition seemed like a good opportunity, and I seized it. Working in the Parking Division with the eventual aim of going into the prisons also meant that I was still laying down the fundamentals for my career and gain-ing financial security while doing it. I was building the road to my independence.

I knew as soon as I started the position that I would no longer be able to accept packages for C. We were out on the streets basically all day—I arrived at my building at 7:30 a.m. and was outside again by 8 o'clock, where I'd spend the next several hours writing parking tickets, before coming back to the building around 4:00 p.m. to turn in my tickets and clock out. The Public Works Department was broadly responsible for the city's road infrastructure—streets, intersections, sidewalks, bikeways—which meant that everyone who worked in the department's various buildings was out and about all day too, fixing potholes or sidewalks or maintaining traffic lights. Because of this, it was almost a guarantee that no one would be around at any of the buildings where we worked to accept packages during the day.

When I told C this, he was kind and accommodating, as usual. He had been ecstatic when I'd first told him that I'd be working in the County Sheriff's Department, and eventually in the jails, thinking that it fit perfectly with the career in criminal psychology I was pursuing. Leaning into the role he liked to play of supportive, understanding partner, he suggested an alternative: "Why don't you ask if Anitra wants to accept the packages?" Using a similar logic he'd given when suggesting Eden, C explained that it would be an easy way for my sister to earn a little extra money. Wrapped around his request were the same assurances he'd given me after Eden's arrest—that the packages this time, and forever going forward, only contained cell phones and pagers; that he would never do anything to jeopardize my career or my family. He knew how close I was to them and knew that my sister and I were especially close.

C knew these things, of course, because we were still talking all the time. The communication between us never stopped. Even throughout the explosive events surrounding Eden and Nate's arrest, our conversations were a constant. Every day, multiple times a day, we were in dialogue—talking, sharing, checking in—commentating about our lives and the occasional dramas that surrounded them, the Eden Incident included. Throughout all of these talks, he blanketed me with reassurances. At every turn he assured me and reassured me, and reassured me some more. These reassurances were always there, at the ready, for him to pull out for whatever conversation called for them. Communication was C's superpower—he used it to calm me; to shower me with love; and ultimately, to redirect me toward only the things he wanted me to see.

Later, during my trial, when I was asked how I could possibly go along with C's request to accept the Beepers Plus packages again after everything that had happened with Eden, how I could get my own sister involved as well, I answered with the most direct truth I could think of:

"I believed him, I honestly did."

I passed C's suggestion on to Anitra, saying he wanted to know if she'd be interested in accepting the boxes of cell phones and pagers. She said she wanted to do it, so I connected the two of them and let C take it from there. In the meantime, I got adjusted to my new routine at the Parking Division, learning the ropes, getting to know my new colleagues. It was a regular job—far from a dream job—but nevertheless it was a step in the right direction for my career.

And then, about a month into my position working as a meter maid, on October 21, 1999, my pager started blowing up toward the end of my shift. Over and over again, C flooded me with "911" messages. When I finally got back to the Parking Division office, I called him back. "Have you talked to your sister?" he asked me. There was a familiar urgency in his voice. "No, why?" I responded. It was the same line of questioning that had begun the Eden drama four months before. "Well, we sent her a package," he explained. Anitra had been accepting the Beepers Plus boxes since I started my new job, but I never knew when they were being sent. C and Anitra had always spoken directly—and my sister and I also barely saw each other at home now. We were on completely opposite schedules: I, working days at the Parking Division, and she, working nights at a bank in Nashville. And so, I had no idea that Anitra was due to receive a package that day. "Then I guess everything is fine, right?" I asked.

"Well, no," C countered. "I haven't talked to Nate, and I called her job, and they said that she's not there. They told me her car is broken down on the side of the road."

Nate. As soon as I heard his name, I knew that something might be up. I hadn't seen or heard from him since he'd gotten out of jail after he was arrested with Eden, but the fact that he'd popped up again to pick up the package that day from my sister set me on edge. C asked me to call Anitra's coworkers at the bank myself to see what they said. The receptionist who answered the phone told me that my sister still hadn't returned to work. She repeated the same story about Anitra's car breaking down on the interstate. Driving home, I kept looking over the guardrail toward the road where they said her car was, searching for her green Chevy Cavalier. If I spotted her, I thought I might be able to pull over and help. But mile after mile, I saw nothing there.

I called her job again as soon as I got back to our house on Granbury. The receptionist told me, once again, that Anitra still hadn't made it back to work yet. I hung up the phone and immediately called Pinky on her cell phone, hoping she might have some news about what was going on. "Have you talked to Pep?"—our nickname for my sister. I was not quite concerned at this point but not totally calm either. "Her job said her car was broken down on the side of the road." Pinky took a bit of a pause before responding.

"Pep's car is not broken down—she's in jail. Something about those damn packages."

I was livid.

———

WHILE MY GRANDMOTHER AND I WERE STILL ON THE PHONE, C BEEPED in on call-waiting to tell me what I already knew. Anitra had been arrested earlier in the day when she went to pick up the packages at a nearby FedEx store in Brentwood. He didn't know there was marijuana in the packages they sent her, he insisted. Travis and Nate went behind his back—*again*—he explained. He didn't know what was going on. He had no idea. He never did. "This is y'all's fault," I cut in before C could say anything more. "You need to fix this. You're going to pay for my sister's bond and get her the fuck out of there."

I couldn't believe what I was hearing—both that Anitra had been arrested and that C was giving me the same explanation for how we ended up in this scenario. Again. I thought, *You can say one time that you didn't know what was going on, but they were able to get around you a second time?* "No way. You're not a dummy, C," I told him, heated. "How am I supposed to believe what you're telling me?" He came back to me with more insisting, more claims of ignorance. More stories I didn't want to hear.

A little while later, Anitra called me from the Williamson County Jail in Franklin, in tears. I told her how sorry I was about what happened, how angry I was at C and Nate—and everyone involved. "You know what I've been charged with?" she asked me. I hadn't gotten any details at that point, just that she'd been taken in, and that Nate had been arrested too. "Possession of marijuana with the intent to distribute." Whatever the amount of marijuana was in those packages, it was definitely more than a joint if the police had determined there was enough to sell. I asked her how much they found inside the boxes. "They said it was thirty-three pounds." Much more than a joint. It was the same amount, in fact, that Eden eventually found out was in the packages the cousins had sent to her.

The pieces were starting to click into place.

I called C and told him that Anitra needed $250 to make her bond, ignoring the empty explanations he continued to try to soften me with, and demanded once again that he give me the funds to get her out. He wired me the money, and Pinky went to pick her up from the Williamson County Jail in Franklin early the next morning.

When I saw her back at the house later that night, my sister gave me the full story of what had happened the day before. Apparently, she'd been caught up in what the police call a "controlled delivery." In instances like these, they catch wind of a drug-filled package being sent through the mail and intercept it before it reaches the recipient. Then, an undercover agent delivers the package instead, disguised as a delivery person. In this case, the packages intended for Anitra to pick up had been flagged by FedEx security when they realized the recipient address did not exist. The boxes had been mislabeled—addressed to 324 Granbury, instead of 325, where we lived. Further examination led FedEx to suspect that the packages contained drugs. They notified the police, who then sent sniffer dogs to the FedEx location in Brentwood, where the boxes were being held, to determine whether there were drugs inside. Which, of course, there were. After this, Travis, Nate, and C were notified by FedEx—now working in collaboration with the police—that their packages were being held for pickup at the Brentwood location on account of the mislabeled shipping address.

On the morning of October 21, Nate called Anitra directly, saying that he needed her to retrieve the boxes from the FedEx store, then meet him at a nearby White Castle to give them to him. "What are you talking about?" Anitra responded. She was caught off guard, she told me, because no one had let her know in advance that a package was being delivered that day, and she was in the middle of a shift at work. It was a Thursday, and she usually received the boxes on Tuesdays and Wednesdays, her days off. Annoyed, Anitra told Nate she wouldn't do it, then hung up the phone. But he kept calling her back, insisting that they needed her to pick up the packages. Anitra was wary of Nate too, having heard about his shady involvement in the Eden arrest. This fact, coupled with Nate's unscheduled, out-of-the-blue ask for a pickup, made my sister hesitate. The only reason she did eventually agree to pick up the packages that day, she told me, was because C called her himself, reassuring her that everything was okay. If I trusted him, Anitra thought, she could too.

On her lunch break, Anitra left work just before noon and headed to the FedEx location to pick up the packages. One of the cousins had called the store that morning to double-check that they were there, and once he got confirmation, he let FedEx know that the recipient (Anitra) was on her way. At the same time, a female undercover agent disguised as a FedEx employee took the cousins' weed-filled boxes from the back room of the store and waited behind the counter for my sister to arrive. Once inside the store, Anitra handed over the tracking number she'd scribbled down on a piece of paper, and the undercover agent gave her one of the boxes. "I think I'm supposed to pick up two?" she told her, and the woman reached behind the counter and gave her the second one.

While carrying the packages back to her car, Anitra got another call from Nate. "Can you tear the labels off?" he asked her. This, she thought, was definitely strange—she had never been asked to do this before. A little confused, but eager to be done with this so she could get back to work, Anitra complied, bending down to peel off each of the labels, and then placed the boxes in the trunk of her car. What she did not know was that the undercover agent behind the FedEx counter was watching her through the store's windows, relaying descriptions of Anitra's appearance and the make and model of her car to other officers stationed nearby. As soon as she lowered the trunk of her car, a flurry of activity exploded around her: sirens wailed, squad cars moved in, and officers surrounded her, yelling "Police!" Their guns were drawn, and they were pointing directly at her.

Back at the station, Anitra was incensed that she'd been caught in the middle of C and Nate's bullshit. When they asked, she told the police she would cooperate and agreed to continue with her scheduled meetup with Nate to deliver the boxes, now as part of an undercover sting operation. She met Nate at the White Castle, as agreed, with the police discreetly positioned close by. But when Nate pulled up with cousin Marcus a few minutes later, Nate said that the scene didn't feel right. Rather than complete the delivery, he asked Anitra to follow him to a different location. They all moved once again—Anitra following Nate, the police following Anitra, this time to an apartment complex parking lot down the road. There, Nate and Marcus finally got the packages out from Anitra's trunk. And as soon as they did, the police moved in.

"I knew I shouldn't have gone and accepted those packages," Anitra repeated to me, anger and regret creeping into her words. She told herself that this pickup was going to be her last; she didn't like dealing with Nate; didn't like the feeling of the whole thing with him involved. "Absolutely," I nodded. "And if I had known that Nate was back in the picture, I would have told you not to do it." Together we began connecting the dots, swapping stories about what she was told, what I was told, what Eden had been told. Nate may have been the warning sign, but this whole web of events extended beyond just him, of course. The connecting point between them, the common denominator for all the chaos that had entered my world in the recent months was C. C with his stories, his explanations, his reassurances. All of which, I was now convinced, were lies.

From that day forward, any trust I placed in C was dead. His words poisoned the air between us.

———

FOLLOWING ANITRA'S ARREST, THE CONVERSATIONS WITH C TRANS-formed from the easy, natural exchanges we'd had since the beginning of our relationship, to a constant push and pull. Pushing for the truth on my end, and pulling away from it on his. I decided that I would keep him close, to make it seem like I still believed in his talk, his version of events, but only to gather as much information as I could to help with the case that was now hanging over my sister's head. Anitra had agreed to cooperate with authorities to help gather information for a larger drug investigation. Finding anything that might be useful to her attorney became the only thing that mattered to me.

C, however, wanted to keep pretending that he knew nothing. That he had never known. That Travis and Nate had always gone behind his back. That all this business with the marijuana was as surprising to him as it was to me. "I lied again," C would later say in his testimony during my trial. "I was continuing to lie." He would eventually admit that he had known all along that his cousins were putting marijuana in the packages, but he never strayed from the story he fed me that he was never directly involved in anything with the drugs. The truth would only be revealed to me much later, during the trial.

Once I figured out that C had no desire to admit his involvement, and that he was not going to give me any useful information to give to my sister, I stopped taking his calls. There was no breakup conversation. There was no "I don't love you anymore; this just isn't working out." I was simply done. There were no more words left to say. No more conversations to be had.

chapter 5

TIME PASSED. ANITRA'S CASE PROGRESSED IN STARTS AND STOPS. SHE would have a court appearance, then not hear anything at all for months, then get called in again for something else. Such is the criminal justice system at work: a series of waiting games, broken up by intermittent—painfully slow—movement. Luckily, my sister could navigate her way through her case from the outside because we had the money to bail her out. But for so many others who can't afford their bond, or don't have anyone to turn to who can pay on their behalf, the only option is to remain in custody. These people stay in jail, month after month—sometimes for a year or more—just waiting for their cases to be resolved.

C still called on and off, but over time he accepted my silence for what it was, and his attempts to contact me eventually stopped. I was barely in my twenties, and felt like I'd accumulated enough life in the last year or so since my relationship with C began to last at least into my thirties. This man had betrayed my trust, not once, but twice. And for that, I had no other choice but to erase him from my life. I scrubbed him from my heart and from my mind and began moving on. *You don't exist to me,* I thought. Then I filed C away for good.

The next two months were relatively uneventful. I woke up early, I worked, I came home. Then I got up and started the next day all over again. As my first six months with the Parking Division were coming to a close, my superiors asked if I would be willing to stay on in the same position for another six months before moving into the jails. I agreed, thankful for another few months of the same reliable schedule.

But a few weeks into the new year, in January 2000, the relative peace I'd been experiencing over the last few months was interrupted. During my shift one day, I was approached by a tall, Black cop who announced himself as Aaron Thomas—a metro police officer assigned to the Twentieth Judicial Drug Task Force in Nashville.

He told me he was working on a drug conspiracy investigation involving Larry and Nate. "I know you know them," he said, literally looking down on me from his height, "and I know what you were doing with them, so just go ahead and tell me." Aaron Thomas was an averagely built man with one gold front tooth and the characteristic demeanor of a cop who seemed to love to use and abuse his power. The metro police officers in Nashville who worked for the drug task force, I would come to learn, had a reputation for treating people terribly, violating their rights and often getting away with it. Aaron Thomas, it turned out, fit this profile to a T. It felt like he had made up his mind that I was guilty before I even opened my mouth to speak, and he wasted no time to treat me like the condemned person he appeared to want me to be.

That day, he looked me up and down and delivered his judgment. He went through some of the events of the last few months, shading them with new, ludicrous inventions that turned the truth into lie after lie. He accused me of setting Eden up that day in June at her mom's apartment. And then, he accused me of setting up my sister too.

"What?" I gave him a look, confused. The words sounded ridiculous coming out of his mouth. "No," I told him repeatedly. "I didn't do either of those things." But he shook off my answers and pressed on, staying his course. He told me that it would only be a matter of time before everything came out, so I might as well come clean now. After a few more minutes of back-and-forth, with him pushing for some admission of guilt he could not find because there was nothing I was guilty of, he finally retreated. But not before threatening my job first. With his initial impression made, he turned to leave. "I'll see you later." He delivered this last part like a promise, his threats and contempt now fully out in the open, as he walked away from me.

While the period immediately following Anitra's arrest may have been quiet for me, for the Nashville Police Department things were just starting to get busy. Larry and Nate had been put on the police's radar back in June, around the time of the Eden Incident, when they connected the dots between Nate's arrest and a string of large sums of money he and Larry had apparently wired from Nashville to California that had been flagged by police as suspicious and possibly drug-related. Then, that October, Nate was arrested again during the sting operation they'd conducted with my sister—heightening their interest in him still further. The police had started to zero in on Nate, and on Travis, and ultimately on C. And because I was C's girlfriend, because I had agreed to do him the favor of accepting packages for what I thought was his family business, the police had also started zeroing in on me.

But of course, I was oblivious to all of this. From where I was standing, C and his cousins' drama had always been theirs alone, and I had separated myself from it entirely the day I cut C out of my life.

I dismissed Aaron Thomas's questions and threats that first day and assumed that would be the end of it.

But in the weeks and months that followed, he kept cropping up like a tenacious patch of weeds. He, along with three other officers he was always with: special agents Paul Conner, Dan Kennedy, and US Federal Prosecutor Sunny Koshy. The four of them rolled together as a pack.

I would see them periodically while I was out writing parking tickets near the Nashville Federal Court House, as they made their way in and out of the building. Our encounters were wordless—they didn't talk to me or attempt to approach; instead, they made their presence known from a distance. Through their hard stares, I got to know their faces: their smug smirks, the way they would size me up with their eyes. Collectively, their presence was oppressive—a dark shadow that sometimes appeared during my workday, a silent reminder that they were watching me.

When I returned home from work on some days, I began seeing them parked not so subtly on the corners near my house, their cars an obvious disruption to the usual scenery of my neighborhood. Because I didn't do anything wrong, their persistent intrusion into my life was all the more infuriating. Like the Franklin cops I noticed in high school who constantly patrolled our neighborhoods for no other reason than to remind us they were there, the Nashville police directed that same energy entirely toward me. I was one person— young, female, and Black—against a much larger, much stronger force, whose intentions, it seemed, were not to serve and protect but to intimidate and harass. To fit me into whatever narrative they had dreamed up and then punish me accordingly.

After several months of this game, during the summer of 2000, the police came to me directly again, this time while I was sitting in my car outside the Public Works building after my shift, preparing to go home. I saw Aaron Thomas cross the street toward me, taking his time as he approached. Knocking on my window, he motioned for me to roll it down. "What do you want?" I said, refusing to be intimidated. I opened the window a crack. He eyed me, looking mildly amused. He said he was there to serve me a subpoena—they wanted my handwriting samples, to match the delivery receipts I signed for the Beepers Plus packages that had been sent to me.

Tired of the antics, I was more than willing to give them whatever they needed so they would leave me alone, once and for all. "Well you can slide it through." I lowered the barrier between us a little more to allow enough space for him to pass the piece of paper to me. He pushed the subpoena through the crack in the window. "You need to be very careful," he said over his shoulder, after he turned to leave. "Because we will mess around and take this pretty little car of yours." I had recently traded in my green Dodge Neon for a white Ford Mustang, paid for with the money I'd saved working the Parking Division job, plus the months of putting money away while working in retail. He walked away without a second look, returning to his car the way he came.

I didn't tell my family about any of this. I didn't tell anyone—not Anitra or Eden or Christana. There was nothing that talking would solve. And so, through it all, I kept moving, continuing on with my life as usual: getting up early, going to work, coming home.

Ignore it and it'll go away, I thought. *If you don't feed it, it don't grow.*

———

BUT IT DID GROW. A COUPLE OF MONTHS AFTER THEY SUBPOENAED ME for writing samples, they began going after Sue Lee as well, who signed for packages on the occasions Anitra or I had boxes sent to her house when we knew we wouldn't be home. My great-grandmother was close to ninety by then, battling colon cancer that had gone in and out of remission, forcing her to endure rounds of chemotherapy and radiation. They served Sue Lee with a subpoena of her own for handwriting samples, demanding that she go to the station and write her name over and over and over again, while Pinky and my two aunts waited for her outside.

Later, after she was recovering from an operation in the hospital when the cancer returned, the Feds appeared again, trying to muscle their way up to her hospital bed to ask her just a few more questions. "You need to leave," Pinky and my aunt Diane told them, matching the officers' stares with their own quiet fury. They left that day without disturbing Sue Lee any further; Pinky and Diane had made it perfectly clear that they were not women to be messed with. That our family was a united front.

This, I think, was the point of realization: when they started harassing my great-grandmother while she was fighting for her life, while we were fighting to keep her with us. In these moments, I realized how far the authorities would go in service of their agenda; how wide a net they would cast to prove a point, however wrong it was.

I *need help*, I told myself, finally, when it became clear that getting some legal advice might be a smart move. I reached out to the law office handling Anitra's case and made an appointment with one of the attorneys there. "They followed you here, too," Glenn Funk told me while I walked him through my story at his office. At one point during our conversation, he'd gotten wind that the Feds—led by Federal Prosecutor Sunny Koshy—were milling around in front of his building, waiting for me to come out. Funk, now Nashville's district attorney general, was then a defense attorney in private practice. He wanted to help, he said, but ultimately he couldn't represent me since my sister's still-open case was being handled by another attorney in his office. Taking me on, Funk said, would be a conflict of interest.

CHAPTER 5

We were standing at the window in his office, overlooking downtown Nashville. "You see that building right across the street?" he asked me, pointing to a grey high-rise about a two-minute walk, I guessed, from where we were. "I want you to go straight over there to see Peter Strianse. I'm going to call and tell him that you're on your way." Peter Strianse was a former federal prosecutor-turned-defense attorney with a stellar track record and the respect of his peers. Funk led me out of his office and walked me to a side door of the building to leave. "A head start," he told me, knowing that the Feds wouldn't be far behind.

I beelined it to Peter Strianse's office, and once inside, I was escorted to a conference room, where he was waiting for me. He gestured for me to have a seat and introduced himself, giving me an empathetic smile. "So, what's going on?" he asked me, leaning forward in his chair. For the first time in a while, it felt like someone was really listening to me—hearing the truth. Shortly after I arrived, Peter got word that the police had followed me to his office too. He excused himself and went down to the lobby, where Sunny Koshy, flanked by several agents, waited by the elevator doors for me to emerge. "Look, she doesn't want to talk to y'all," Peter told them, blown away by the aggressive tactics they were resorting to in order to approach me. "It's not going to happen. I don't care if she has to stay here all day."

He would later describe the entire scene as bizarre—an over-the-top, totally inappropriate display of intimidation that didn't go over well with him at all. And he told them as much. Realizing they were not going to get what they wanted, Koshy and his agents eventually packed up and left.

Peter and I had a good talk, but when it came down to the question of next steps, I thought hiring him at that point might be a little premature. He would cost $25,000, which I knew my family didn't have. And retaining him seemed unwarranted, considering I had done nothing wrong. I was still sure that all the evidence and common sense supporting my innocence would ultimately cross me off the Feds' list.

I left Peter's office that day with his card in my pocket, hoping I would never have to use it.

chapter 6

THINGS DIED DOWN AGAIN. ENOUGH FOR ME TO BELIEVE THAT THE investigation had finally moved past me. The Feds' presence had faded, the oppressive atmosphere lifted, and I no longer worried about running into Sunny Koshy or Aaron Thomas—or the rest of their crew—while trying to live my life day-to-day. My second six months with the Parking Division was ending, which meant that it was time to start my position as a correctional officer (CO) in the jails. I told myself that after six to eight months there, I would return to TSU to finish out my criminal psychology degree, knowing that this kind of on-the-ground experience would count for the essential internship credits I needed for graduation.

All new classes of COs had to complete six weeks of training before going inside. It was an intense, physically draining program that involved learning hand-to-hand combat and joint manipulation techniques through hapkido, a Korean martial art. A major component of the training was an obstacle course, which ended with being sprayed in the face with the kind of mace we had to be certified to use. We stood in a line as our superiors spritzed it onto us like perfume, before continuing through the last stretch of the course. We had to keep moving for many minutes while the chemical was in full effect. When it dried, the mace crystalized and often got stuck to our eyebrows, which meant that when we showered later, it melted and trickled down our faces, burning all over again. In some ways, it almost felt like we were being prepared for war: "us," the officers, the authority figures, versus "them," the population we were tasked to "control."

I had never been inside a jail before in my life—I had never even seen movies or read books about life inside jails—so I had no idea what to expect. But having spent the last several years eager to work with and study people who had committed crimes, I was excited to jump into the unknown. I was officially entering the world I'd always wanted to explore.

I did my on-the-job training at the three main detention facilities in Nashville: first, at the Male Correctional Development Center (CDM) at Harding Place, the lowest-level custody jail; then a turn at the Hill Detention Center (HDC), which contained mostly medium-security inmates; then, finally, at the Criminal Justice Center (CJC), the city's highest-level custody jail and also by far its worst.

CJC, which was demolished in 2017 to make way for a new maximum-security jail complex, was a square, five-story brick building that was deteriorating from the inside and out after decades of overuse. Walking in my first day there, I immediately noticed how dark it was. The lighting inside all the jails was entirely without warmth—the facilities were always either flooded with harsh, bright light or very dimly lit. The cold extended to the air itself; it was freezing inside, always. The temperature was kept low, I was told, to reduce the spread of germs. The walls at CJC were filthy, caked with layers of peeling paint, and the floors were crawling with roaches and other insects that had found their way inside. *This is no way to live,* I thought when I walked around, getting to know the concrete rooms, the halls lined with metal bars.

And then there was the smell. There are things that are specific to these places that are often hard to put into words, and "jail smell" is one of those things. It was present in all of the jails I worked in during my training. It hits you immediately, and it is unmistakable. It follows you home, it gets in your hair, and in your nose, and in your clothes. Ask anyone who's been inside a jail or prison, and they'll likely tell you the same thing.

After training, I cycled back to the Male Correctional Development Center, the lowest-level security jail, where I would spend the rest of my tenure as a CO. I worked in the E and F pods—the pretrial units, which consisted of folks who had been arrested but not yet convicted of the crimes they'd been accused of. Most of the men there were low-level, nonviolent offenders: homeless people, low-income people who couldn't make bond, undocumented people the police had rounded up. In other words, CDM was filled to the brim with individuals—*overwhelmingly* Black and brown—who were criminalized and incarcerated because of their circumstances.

Each unit housed about sixty inmates in a big, open room filled with bunk beds. Our job was to patrol our units and keep the peace—which, I quickly learned, essentially came down to the babysitting of grown men. We were tasked with enforcing when they ate and when they slept. When they made their beds and did their laundry. We monitored all of their activities, all of their movements, to ensure that they were "staying in line."

They're already locked up, I thought, when the directive was drilled into us for the millionth time. *How much more "in-line" could they be?*

But for my colleagues—mostly white guys, save for a couple of other Black officers that I became cool with—this kind of close monitoring bred the power dynamic they grew to crave. We were never taught how to interact with those imprisoned during our training, beyond how to establish our authority, and how to secure the facility should a situation get out of control. "Respect" was a word applied in theory—we were, of course, told to treat the people held inside the jails with civility. But in practice, I saw just how quickly that idea got tossed out of the window once many of the officers got a taste of what their power could do—the advantages it gave them, the control they could wield. Power was the card they most liked to play. The fact that most of the inmates on the receiving end of their power were Black and brown was something that I did not understand the full weight of at the time—not even close. I didn't have the context then.

I didn't know that the origins of modern-day policing stretch all the way back to slavery, when militia groups were formed to hunt down runaway enslaved people, and then later to enforce discriminatory Southern Black Codes and Jim Crow laws that sought to strip Black people of their freedoms. I didn't have the numbers either. I didn't know that a Black person is five times more likely than a white person to be stopped without just cause; that while African Americans and Latinos make up 32 percent of the US population, they represent over half—56 percent—of the prison population. I didn't know that if these same folks were incarcerated at the same rates as white people, prison and jail populations in America would decline by almost 40 percent. I didn't know any of these things. But I did know, in my bones, that what I was seeing, day after day, was wrong.

I witnessed many of the officers I worked with thriving on their power trips—yelling at inmates, demeaning them, getting in their faces and instigating fights, just so they could call a "code" for assistance, prompting a mob of officers to rush in and take the inmates down. It was that same air of arrogance and untouchability that I'd seen, over and over again, in Aaron Thomas and his crew. Working alongside my fellow new recruits, I saw up close how that mentality was born. We may have been taught one thing in the academy, but as soon as many of the officers stepped foot inside a jail, the allure of having so much to lord over another person—of being able to act with impunity behind the safety of a uniform—was too much for them to resist. And why would they resist, when many of the seasoned correctional officers—men who had been working in jails for decades—used and abused their power too. In this way, the toxic culture in the jails was nurtured and spread, by unspoken permission, from one CO to the next. It was a normal, everyday part of their environment. One I refused to participate in.

Lucky for me, when you're in charge of your pods, you mostly work alone, so I could create the culture of my own space. I knew immediately that I would do things differently. I would treat the men who were put in these jails like they deserved to be treated—as people, not like animals trapped in a cage.

The ecosystem of jails is structured around three shifts: first shift, between 7 a.m. and 2 p.m.; second shift, between 2 p.m. and 11 p.m.; and third shift, between 11 p.m. and 7 a.m. During the day, there's constant movement: Nurses are going around to pass out meds; people are entering, being classified, or leaving jail. Inmates are watching TV in the day room, or talking on the phones, or taking showers. COs pass around lunch, then dinner. And finally toward the end of the day, the rock men—the inmates who work outside their cells preparing meals in the kitchen or cleaning up around the facility—begin making their way back to their units.

I primarily worked the late night/early morning third shift, which means that my "day" began long after most of the peak activity had died down. Save for the period when we handed out breakfast or got that day's list of inmates ready for court—waking them up, handing out razors for them to shave with—the hours during third shift passed quietly. Once every thirty minutes, we had to make rounds throughout our areas, circling the pods to ensure that nobody was doing anything they weren't supposed to do, then mark that we'd successfully completed the round in our log books. But after that, our time was largely ours to manage. Many of the other officers chose to spend their downtime together, but not me. With the exception of a few whom I got along with, I had no desire to interact with the other officers any more than I had to. I chose to spend the slow stretches of time alone instead or, more often than not, chatting with the inmates.

I started getting to know the guys in my pods, talking to them and listening to their stories. "Ms. Haynes, you got a minute?" they'd often say, whenever I'd pass by. They talked to me about their cases— so many of which, I learned, were for trivial, minor offenses like trespassing or vandalism. We talked about the things they wanted to do and people they wanted to be when they got out. But mostly, we just talked about life. In a place that hostile and isolating, a lot of the guys just wanted somebody to listen. And I, quite literally, was going to be there all night. So, I thought, might as well pass the time together. What harm would it cause me to listen to whatever these guys had to say?

I remember one person in particular with whom I had a lot of these kinds of conversations. He was a young kid, Black, maybe eighteen years old—only a few years younger than me. I don't even remember why he was in there; we didn't discuss his case very much. But we did talk a lot about what he was going to do when he got out. "I'm going to get my life together Ms. Haynes," he would tell me. "I'm not trying to be in and out of jail." The pretrial pods were overflowing with similar stories: young Black men who got caught up in the system and feared the revolving door of incarceration that threatened to take them down—the unfair targeting by the police; the bail that might be too high to pay; the harsher charges inevitably facing them, simply for existing in the bodies they were born in.

There was another guy around my age whom I also remember well, a white kid the other inmates called "Red" because of his rust-colored hair. Red was different from many of the other guys in my pods because his case wasn't low level; he was being held on a federal drug case. He would talk about his situation some, about the federal system, and especially about "mandatory minimums"—the sentencing laws that required automatic minimum prison terms for certain crimes, particularly ones involving drugs. He was waiting out his conviction on drug conspiracy charges that involved a big group of people, many of whom he barely knew.

I couldn't have known then just how familiar this concept would become for me; how it would impact my own life soon enough.

Month after month, I learned the inmates' stories, earning their trust and respect. Unlike many of the other officers, I saw no difference between me and the men I was hired to patrol, except that we existed on two different sides of freedom. They were people, like you and me, and I was determined to lead with their humanity first. They were already locked up, stripped of all sense of normality, of the comfort and enjoyment they got from their regular routines. So if they wanted to, say, get off their bunks on a Friday night after I was finished making my rounds, why should I care? Creating some semblance of regular life in a place that would never be regular became my goal. I started finding that it made my job—and their experience—much more tolerable.

Whenever new people came in and attempted to try me—seeing this young girl they thought would be an easy target—the guys who knew me well would come to my defense. "No, that's Ms. Haynes. We don't do that with her," they'd say. "She's cool." In the months

I spent at the Male Correctional Development Center—often as the only woman authority figure in a room of men—I never felt scared or threatened. I never had a problem with any of the guys incarcerated there. I never had to call a code for backup. I never had to compromise myself or my principles in order to adhere to some standard of law and order that I inherently didn't agree with.

I entered the jails as someone interested in learning more about why people charged with crimes do what they do. But I left with a different set of questions that needed answering. Hearing so many of the inmates' stories, I started thinking differently about exactly *who* was in prison, and *why* they were actually there. I couldn't ignore the types of people I saw being processed in the jails day after day, week after week. So many of the people crowding my pods were there simply because they didn't have a home or the right documentation, or because they couldn't afford bail for some inconsequential arrest a cop could have just as easily let them walk free on. And as a result, they were there with me, languishing inside a concrete and metal pod instead of living their lives.

I started to doubt whether I still wanted to study criminal behavior or work with serial killers, as had been my dream for so many years. Now, I was consumed with a new thought: *What can I do to prevent people from coming to jail in the first place? From having to experience . . . this?*

Months later, after I had stopped working in the jails and returned to school at TSU, I was crossing the parking lot of a restaurant with a few of my friends when I heard someone yelling my name, "Hey! Ms. Haynes!" I turned my head in the direction I heard the call coming from and immediately recognized who it was: the eighteen-year-old Black kid who talked so much with me about his life plans after he got out of jail. He walked up to me, beaming; gave me a hug and told me that he had been doing good. "I'm glad to hear it," I responded, and I genuinely was. It was a quick conversation, no more than a couple of minutes. But it made me happy that he was out, walking free.

Back then, the encounter was just a nice end to the story—a happy moment with someone I once knew, which occurred during the course of a night out with friends. An exchange that happened in passing, but not something I thought much about afterward. But when I think back on that memory now, frustration also pushes its way through. Knowing, as I know now, that there was so much more the criminal justice system could have done for that kid than locking him up. Knowing that we live in a society in which the first and foremost punitive action we face, especially for people who look like me, is to be locked away.

In the years to come, I would hear again someone call out my name in a parking lot, or from across the street, or inside a store. Every time I heard, "Ms. Haynes! Ms. Haynes!" I knew exactly who it was and what that person had overcome to get to where they were, on the outside. The cycle, now, is all too familiar to me. The reality that for people of color—for Black men and boys, for Black women and girls—the odds never seemed to be in our favor.

Even so, whenever I ran into one of these guys, I always hoped for good news.

RESUMED MY STUDIES AT TSU WITH A DIFFERENT SENSE OF MY PATH. I wanted to get back out into the real world as soon as possible to begin tackling the questions that I had started to think about during my time as a correctional officer in the jails. A career in criminal psychology, I realized, would require at least a PhD to do anything useful, which meant *years* more schooling than I was willing to put in. But pursuing a degree in criminal justice with a minor in psychology could place me closer to what I now wanted—to really *study* the criminal justice system—and I could reach this goal in far less time.

Needing electives to fulfill my new criminal justice major, I signed up, on a whim, for a class called "Legal Methods"—mostly because it fit around my job schedule. I had resumed doing retail again, working as an assistant manager at Charlotte Russe at the Opry Hills Mall in Nashville in between my full-time course load at school. The Legal Methods class was taught by Larry Woods, a middle-aged, salt-and-pepper–haired white professor, who had been practicing law for some time. Paging through the syllabus he passed around on the first day of class, I was surprised to see that every assignment for

the semester consisted solely of law cases we were supposed to review—no fewer than four cases per class. Completely unbeknownst
to me, I had enrolled in a prelaw course—and not an introductory
one. It was filled mostly with students who had their sights firmly
set on law school.

For each case, we were told by Professor Woods to submit something called a "brief." I had no idea what a brief was, but I assumed
it was just a summary of information. *Easy enough*, I thought. I began
working on my first assignment feeling confident about the outcome,
thoroughly reading the case, then providing a blow-by-blow of all
the major plot points. But a week later, when the brief was returned
to me with a less than stellar grade, I realized I might have underesti-
mated what was being asked of me. I totally bombed the assignment.
"Come see me during office hours," Professor Woods wrote at the
top of my paper. I had been a high achiever throughout most of my
academic career, and I wasn't about to let this class be my undoing, so
I went to his office, ready to figure out how to fix what was going on.

During our meeting, Professor Woods took the time to explain
the concept of a brief in more detail, breaking it down into each
of its elements: the issue, the rule, the application of the rule, and
the conclusion. In a comprehensive document, which could consist
of hundreds of pages of information, the brief is meant to distill
the case down to its essence. It was all about determining what was
important and what was not, what you needed and what you didn't
need, then drilling down on the most essential facts to illuminate the
argument. Something clicked when Professor Woods explained it to
me this way. I had always been curious about the "why?" of things.
And in a way, a brief was just an extension of that investigation. It
took a legal case and organized it into clearly defined components so
that someone could more easily determine how court decisions were
made, and what logic was used to make them.

CHAPTER 7

From that day forward, writing briefs became second nature to me. I loved sorting through all the facts, rooting out the crucial pieces, and synthesizing everything into one succinctly worded page. I remember one case we were instructed to brief laid out the argument for a patient's right to die—whether the family of a child who lost all brain function could remove her from life support; or if it was the hospital's responsibility to keep her alive, regardless of the family's wishes. The argument came down to who, ultimately, had the right to prolong a life: The family? The doctors? The court system? When I got my grade back on the assignment, Professor Woods told me that it was the best brief he'd received in all his years teaching at TSU.

Still, even though I could have had all the right answers and un- derstood the assignments inside and out, I was never going to be the student to raise my hand in class or to be the leader of group discussions. But I did my work and I did it well. I was on the Dean's List and consistently excelled on my homework. In discovering this class, I had found my niche. At first, it was just the concept of brief- ing cases that interested me. Then, it became about getting to know different aspects of the law. I loved reading through the legal doc- uments assigned to us and taking the time to dig deeper into their meanings. There was something about knowing that, on an essential level, our laws were put in place to help people, and in understand- ing them, I could defend and advocate for those who needed that kind of help most. I read about all the amendments contained in the Constitution—all of the rights they were created to protect—and began to understand deeply what these amendments truly meant.

Slowly, I started to realize that perhaps what I really wanted to do was practice law, specifically criminal defense law. When I was working in jails, it was all about humanizing people, making sure they were being treated with the dignity and respect they deserved, regardless of why they were there or what someone said they had done. In choosing the path of a criminal defense attorney, I could fight to protect those the law was designed to protect. I could make sure people's rights were not violated.

Before long, I was seriously contemplating law school. *Maybe University of Florida*, I thought, excited by the idea of living and studying near the beach. I took the idea to Professor Woods one day after class in his office. "University of Florida would be lucky to have you," he told me. "But you should really consider Harvard or Yale." The suggestion of going to an Ivy League school caught me off guard. I had never considered it, and I didn't think I could compete with kids who had probably lived and breathed in elite spaces since the day they were born. "You can handle it," Professor Woods reassured me. But I wasn't convinced that that was the kind of career path I truly wanted. Still, the seed of law school had been planted, and I began pursuing that new goal.

And then, I started seeing the same unwelcome familiar faces again, lurking around the corners of my life: the Feds, led by Sunny Koshy and the rest of his irritating crew.

I would see them parked throughout the neighborhood near my house, conspicuously within view. At one point, I even spotted Sunny Koshy at the mall, sitting in the food court near my store. He came inside and walked around, without saying a word to me, and then abruptly left the same way he had come. Nothing about this was normal. Or standard practice. Or the typical course of procedure. Nothing about them following me around, showing up at my job or harassing my family, was a necessary part of conducting their investigation. "Extremely, extremely unusual," Peter had called it, reflecting later on the day the Feds had followed me into his office, waiting by the elevators for me to leave so they could bombard me with questions once again. It was intimidation, plain and simple. A show of strategically displayed force—the Feds' constant presence there to remind me that they could use or withhold their power at will, whenever and however they felt the need.

Not long after, they served me a second subpoena to complete another round of handwriting samples. Once again, I sat in a big, empty room inside the Nashville federal building and signed my name, over and over again, on a piece of paper: *Keeda J. Haynes, Keeda J. Haynes, Keeda J. Haynes, Keeda J. Haynes.*

While I was there, I was also approached by agent Dan Kennedy, playing the role of "good cop" in the roster of bad ones who had been bothering me on and off for so many months. He wanted to talk to me about the investigation. "Listen, I'm just trying to do my job," he said, pretending empathy and understanding. "You help me out, I'll help you out." I agreed to do it. I had nothing to hide, and nothing—or so I thought, anyway—to lose.

I offered Dan Kennedy what I knew, to the best of my limited knowledge: That C had asked me to accept packages containing cell phones and pagers. That Nate or Larry would pick them up either from my house, or my great-grandmother's house, or sometimes from my job. That I signed for them, always, using my name, Keeda J. Haynes. And that I had no reason to believe that there weren't cell phones and pagers in the boxes that were sent me. I had no idea that there was marijuana in the boxes. I told Kennedy my recollection of events on the day Eden was arrested, and about the period of time afterward when I stopped receiving packages, before eventually agreeing to accept them again because C told me repeatedly that everything was fine. And then I told him about how C got my sister involved too and about her arrest. I told the truth as I had always understood it. The "truth" as it was fed to me by C.

Around the same time, C was also brought in to talk with the Feds about the investigation. After not speaking to him at all in well over a year, I was surprised to see his name on my caller ID, ringing my cell phone out of the blue. "I miss you," he told me. "I miss hearing your voice." He said he was in Nashville for the interview and wanted to know if he could see me. His threadbare stories were so transparent to me now—it was obvious that his attempt to reconnect was just a ploy to get information out of me ahead of his meeting. I was sure that he wanted to get a better sense of what I knew. "No, C," I replied, not trusting the words coming out of his mouth. "I can't see you." I hung up the phone, and, as an extra measure, I changed my number. He was the last person I wanted to allow access to me.

There were no lawyers, cameras, or tape recorders present during the day Dan Kennedy interviewed me at the Nashville federal building. His official report was made simply from a summary of his own notes. In it, he took the facts I gave him and twisted my words into the narrative the government had been pushing all along, portraying me not as someone unknowingly caught up in somebody else's wrongdoing, but as a deliberate coconspirator in the entire scheme.

My name was added to a list of twenty-eight people formally indicted in a large-scale drug conspiracy, spearheaded in large part by C and by his cousins. Two days later, the Feds surrounded my house to arrest me.

chapter 8

I WAS FINISHING UP A FRIDAY EVENING SHIFT AT CHARLOTTE RUSSE when I got the call. "Baby you need to come home," my mother said, calmly. "They've come here looking for you." I stood there, still, listening to what she was telling me. "And be careful," she added, before I had a chance to respond. "Because we don't know where they are." I called my good friend Joy and told her what my mother had just told me, and she suggested that I come over to her house in Franklin so that she could follow me to my own house in her car— just in case I ran into any trouble along the way. I drove the thirty minutes back to Franklin and stopped at Joy's place. We talked for a bit when I got there, then returned to our cars and drove the short remaining distance, turning onto Granbury Street and then parking in front of my house.

When I walked in, Pinky and my mom were sitting in the living room, waiting for me. They said that just before my mom called me at work, the police had shown up at the house, knocking on the front door. When she and Pinky opened it, they were greeted by a fully outfitted SWAT team. They had surrounded the area, positioning themselves out front and around the corner of the house. My mom and Pinky also heard helicopters flying overhead. "Is Keeda Haynes in there?" the police asked, voices raised to be heard over the loud whir of the helicopters. "No, she's not," Pinky responded. "Well, where is she?" they shot back, demanding more than asking. Standing squarely in the doorway, unshaken by the theatrics on display in front of her, my grandmother told them she didn't know where I was. The Feds just stood there, facing my grandmother down, waiting for her to say more. "You want to come in here and look for her yourself?" she said finally, after a few long moments of silence. They shook their heads and told her no. Then they turned around, packed up the whole scene, and left. That's when my mother picked up her phone and called me, telling me to come home—and to be careful because they were looking for me.

After she and I hung up and I was on my way back to Franklin, Pinky rang Roy Brown, a long-time Franklin police officer, who also happened to be a good friend of the family. She told him what had just transpired with the Feds outside the house and asked for his advice. "Pinky, y'all just go ahead and bring Keeda in," he told her. "It'd be better to bring her in than having them find her and arrest her."

Sitting next to her and my mama in the living room, my grandmother relayed all of this news to me in the grounded, matter-of-fact manner that was her way. *This is the situation, and it is what it is.* I don't remember at all now how I was feeling or what I was thinking, but I can't imagine that I really understood what was unfolding—there was no way I could have. I still thought this was a misunderstanding that could be worked out. That announcing myself at the police station would bring me a step closer to getting my name cleared once and for all. I changed out of my work clothes and went down to the Williamson County Police Station, ready to finally be done with this nonsense. Thinking, in the absolute worst-case scenario, that maybe I'd have to post bond before being told I was free to go.

But it didn't happen like that. It didn't turn out that way at all.

———

THAT FRIDAY NIGHT, I WAS BOOKED INTO THE WILLIAMSON COUNTY Jail, where I would remain throughout the entire weekend. It was my first time back at a jail since I left my position as a correctional officer—only this time I was on the other side of the system.

After being processed, every new inmate was given a dingy green mattress and told to set it up on an open bunk in any pod they wanted—it didn't matter where. While I was dragging my mattress across the concrete floor, searching for a place to put it, I suddenly heard someone say: "Keeda Haynes? Is that Keeda Haynes?" I knew it wasn't one of the people I'd met as a correctional officer because this was clearly the voice of a woman, and all of the people in my pods had been men. *Who is calling my name in jail?* I asked myself, looking around to find the source. My eyes landed on a blonde-haired, blue-eyed white girl—a cheerleader-type. She was looking at me, as shocked as I was, from across the room.

"Heather Goodman?" I immediately recognized her. Heather was a year behind me at Franklin High School.

"What are you doing here?!" Heather exclaimed.

"No . . ." I responded, still looking at her, stunned. "What the hell are *you* doing here?"

Holed up together in the Williamson County Jail, Heather and I talked. I found out that she was there on a conspiracy drug charge as well—also because of a shady boyfriend who got her involved in something without divulging what she was truly getting involved in. Sunny Koshy, that bully of a federal prosecutor who had orchestrated the intimidation I'd been experiencing over the last few months, was working Heather's case too. "That man is pure evil," she warned me, detailing her own experiences with him. She gave me the lowdown on how badly the government had treated her and her boyfriend. How wide a net they often cast when they were prosecuting conspiracy drug charges, scooping up anyone who may have been even peripherally involved—knowingly or not—in the operation they were getting busted for. Despite Heather's family having the money for bail—had that option been on the table—the courts weren't letting her out. She'd been sitting in jail for months awaiting trial, she told me.

Speaking with Heather Goodman was my first big eye-opener to what might be in store for me. In hearing her story, I saw what could very possibly be my future—being wrapped up in something much bigger than me; punished unfairly for a crime I didn't commit; in serious trouble, all because of the lies of some man and because of the government's refusal to hear the truth.

At some point during the weekend I called home, totally overwhelmed by the last few days. My mama answered the phone, listening to me recount stories about the conditions, the food, the state I was in, as I fought back tears. "Well, we got some good news," she told me.

"What—I'm getting out?" A bit of hope rising up in my chest. "No, we hired Peter Strianse." The defense attorney whose legal advice I'd sought several months before; the one who told the investigators who had followed me inside his office that they had to leave. Apparently, we would be needing Peter after all.

———

THAT MONDAY MORNING, THE MARSHALS PICKED ME UP AND TOOK ME to the courthouse in downtown Nashville, where I was scheduled to make my initial appearance. In the federal system there are statutes in the law that say if you're charged with certain offenses, the government can recommend that you be detained because you're deemed a danger to the community. What I was being charged with, drug conspiracy, fell under one of those detainable offenses, and Sunny Koshy filed a motion to keep me in custody. To contest the motion, Peter had to successfully argue that I was not, indeed, a public safety risk, and to do that, we had to have a detention hearing.

I was told that I would be waiting out my days before the hearing date was set in Warren County Regional Jail, about an hour away, in Bowling Green, Kentucky. They led me out of the courtroom and walked me to the back of the marshal's office, where I sat in a small holding cell—alone—for the rest of the day while I waited to be taken to Kentucky. Hours passed without anyone coming by to tell me what was going on. The only way I knew I wasn't in there entirely by myself was because there was a door that led back to the office, and every once in a while I heard keys jingling or the sounds of the comings and goings of whoever was on the other side of the door. But by five or six o'clock, everyone in the office seemed to have left for the day. As it got quieter and quieter, I grew more concerned that I might have to spend the rest of the night by myself in this holding cell. I thought, for sure, that I had been forgotten.

At around seven o'clock that night—after having been in the federal building since at least nine that morning—the guards finally came in to the cell, cuffing me again to transport me to Bowling Green.

Warren County Regional Jail was awful—just as bad as the conditions I had observed during my correctional officer training at CJC in Nashville—with its filthy walls and peeling paint. I was instructed to remove my street clothes and get dressed in a red, standard-issue jail uniform; I was then sent into a pod with an itchy wool blanket that gave me a rash. The room was designed to hold maybe eight women, but there were always at least ten to twelve of us in there, many sleeping on mattresses on the floor because there weren't enough bunks. Smoking inside the pod was allowed, and the smell of cigarettes clung to everything—suffocating the air, seeping deep into my clothes and hair, working its way into the blankets, affecting the taste of the food.

The food at Warren had its own set of issues, though. Primarily, it was disgusting. I could barely keep down the powdered eggs they gave out—a yellow blob of matter that I only attempted to eat because after a while, I had to try to eat something. I got sick a few times as a result, and I barely ate a thing for the rest of the time I was there. With the constant cloud of cigarette smoke and that scratchy blanket I was allergic to, I barely slept while I was there, either. I thought that I would only be in Warren for a night or two, but I ended up being stuck there for about a week before someone finally came to tell me that it was time to go back to Nashville for my detention hearing. I was dressed in my regular clothes—the same ones I wore when I turned myself in in Franklin—then placed in a police van, handcuffed and shackled for the entire hour-long ride back to the Nashville federal building.

When Peter and I stood in front of the judge to argue for my release, we soon discovered that there was no need. Sunny Koshy had withdrawn his motion to detain me on the date of the initial court appearance—*days* before—knowing that I would have to sit in jail for an extra few days until Peter had returned from a planned trip out of town. Peter had told them when he would be gone when they were setting the initial hearing date, which consequently had to be moved. I personally believed that stewing in jail, letting the system work me over, was a tactic that Koshy hoped would scare me into pleading guilty. He was far from the only one in his line of work who did these kinds of things to the people they were trying to bend and break to help their own cases.

CHAPTER 8

I was released from jail that day on my own recognizance—which is rare in the federal system, particularly if you have a drug offense, and *especially* if you are Black—and returned to the custody of my family. Shortly thereafter, I set up an appointment with Peter to begin preparing for what would come next.

———

PART OF THE TERMS OF MY RELEASE WAS THAT I STAY IN SCHOOL AND also continue to work—two things I was committed to doing regardless. To make sure I was complying with the court's requirements, I had to check in regularly with a pretrial release service officer. Once a month I called Paul Montgomery, a nice, even-tempered Black man who treated me fairly and with respect—a sharp contrast from the government officials I'd dealt with so far during this process. He'd ask me how I was doing, how classes and work were, and at the end of each semester I'd send him a copy of my school transcripts.

Considering the circumstances, these check-ins were relatively painless. At worst, they were another annoying set of assurances I had to submit myself to in order to prove what I already knew—that I was a regular, responsible college student who had done nothing wrong. But then came the day when Paul called me to say that I would have to do a drug test. His supervisors were going through the paperwork on my case and noticed that I hadn't been tested for drugs since they released me—another common requirement for pretrial release. He knew it was unnecessary, he told me, but those were the rules.

Once again I made my way down to Nashville's federal building and submitted myself to what would be another round of humiliation. With mirrors surrounding the toilet in the bathroom, I peed into a plastic cup while an expressionless white woman leaned against the door and watched, saying nothing. Have you ever experienced a stranger watching you pee like it was her job? It's dehumanizing—to be monitored, scrutinized, and judged while you are literally all out there, exposed. I know now that scenarios like these are just part of what the system does to keep you feeling like you are less than. It's another example in a long line of tactics deployed to intimidate, to keep certain people in their place. I had no drug or alcohol history to speak of, but I still had to be subjected to a drug test, regardless of what the facts of my life added up to. Sitting on the toilet, watching this woman watching me, I couldn't even imagine what it must be like for people who had to experience this on a regular basis. Having to do it once was more than enough for me.

On top of these check-ins with Paul, I was also meeting regularly with Peter to prepare my case. "I'm going to do what you want me to," he told me during our first meeting. "If you say you want to take a plea, I'll talk to them and we'll work it out. If you say you want to go to trial, we'll go to trial. I'm not afraid of that—I've been to trial many times before."

From the very beginning, I knew that negotiating a plea deal was not going to be an option for me. It went against everything I was to admit guilt when I was innocent. This was essentially what a plea deal came down to: cop to at least some part of the crimes you're being accused of, and avoid or reduce your jail time. I just couldn't do it. Plus, law school was becoming more and more of a reality for me. I knew that there was only a slim chance of me being able to practice law with a felony on my record.

And so, the path forward for me was clear: I was going to go to trial.

From that day on, the only time Peter and I talked about pleas was whenever the prosecution team came to him with another offer—and there were many in the months leading up to my court date. Every time a new plea deal came in, Peter would say, "I know we've talked about this, and I know where you stand, but it's my obligation as your attorney to share it with you." He would convey the offer to me, and I would deny it, then we would keep on moving, preparing for trial.

Our biggest task was going through all of the discovery—or the state's evidence in the drug conspiracy case—which was a lot, since twenty-eight of us in total had been indicted. Up until that point, I had only been afforded small slivers of the picture—what C had admitted to me when I pressed him for answers years before, or what I'd pieced together myself despite his lies. But contained within the mountain of documents spread out between Peter and me in his office was the full scope of C and his cousins' deception. "Discovery," I realized, was quite a fitting word for everything I was looking at.

There was so much that I was learning for the first time: the logistics of how C and his cousins ran the operation; all the things they'd kept from me, and from my sister, and from Eden. The abundance of information—and the extent of the whole scheme—it was eye-opening. *No wonder they got caught,* I thought, scanning document after document. I had already known that C was lying, but now the full scale of it—all the actors, all the many moving parts—was unfolding in front of my eyes on these pages.

The conspiracy had happened, that part was abundantly clear. Peter's focus for the trial was proving all the ways in which I had no knowledge of what was really going on. So, we went over everything, piece by piece, to try to get a sense of what the other side might say, and how they would try to lay out how the conspiracy had happened, implicating me.

We practiced direct-examination and cross-examination with one of Peter's colleagues, Kim Hodde. They would review all the questions Peter would ask me during the trial, then Kim would play Sunny Koshy, asking things they thought he might bring up. Sitting across from me at a long table in one of Peter's conference rooms,

Kim acted as obnoxious as she could manage, knowing this was how Sunny would perform in the courtroom. She hurled her questions at me, adding little snide comments meant to get under my skin. Peter wanted me to be prepared for any of the snarky-ness, or the rudeness, or the disrespect that Sunny Koshy would no doubt come at me with.

These days were exhausting—the whole process of the case was—but I also still had to keep up with my full schedules, both at school and at work. It was a surreal parallel: dissecting law cases with Professor Woods in class, then leaving school and going over my own case in preparation for my trial.

Professor Woods knew what was going on—the case had started getting some media attention, and my name had appeared in a few newspaper articles. We'd talked about it once or twice, and I remember it coming up one day during a conversation we were having after class.

"They've got to see you as a nineteen-year-old girl, Keeda. Not the twenty-two-year-old you are now," he told me. Professor Woods knew who I was—he knew that I was smart and on the ball; that I had good grades and things going for me. But he also knew that the biggest hurdle when it came to the trial was convincing people that I didn't know what was in those packages. "People need to see you as you were then, not as you are now." He suggested that I play down my strength; that I make myself smaller to appear more naïve. I listened to what Professor Woods was saying, taking everything in. But I also wasn't quite sure that the me of the past, when I'd first met C, and the me in the present were so different. I had always been assertive—then, at nineteen, and certainly now, at twenty-two. In my gut, I knew that when I was sitting up there on the stand, I couldn't be anybody else.

CHAPTER 8

With all of this advice and preparation swirling around me, I inched my way toward the trial date. I was as ready as I was going to be. But even with all the examination and cross-examination run-throughs with Peter, all the rehearsing of what the other side might say or do, looking back, I don't think there's any amount of practice that prepares you to face down a system that is trying to take away your liberty. Or the people who are accusing you of doing things you absolutely did not do. You can certainly try to prepare someone. You can say, "You should answer the question this way"; "You should do this or that"; "Don't let them rile you up." But at the end of the day, it's *your* liberty, your freedom, that's on the line.

I was preparing to battle for my life. And so, no matter what, I wasn't going to back down.

chapter 9

O N APRIL 30, 2002, THE PROCEEDINGS OF UNITED STATES V. KEEDA Haynes began.

By the time I walked into the courtroom that first day of trial—thirteen months after the initial indictment came down—every single one of my twenty-seven codefendants had succumbed to taking a plea deal. Everyone, that is, except for me. While Sunny Koshy and his investigators had deployed similar bullying tactics on each of them—threatening their kids, their homes, and their freedom to obtain an admission of guilt—I refused to give in.

I was the lone person in the entire group implicated in the conspiracy who would be arguing my innocence in front of a judge and jury.

The trial kicked off with opening statements. Sunny Koshy went first, detailing all of the major turns in the case—the entire course of C and his cousins' drug activity—beginning well before I had even met C. He went over everything—my acceptance of the packages, Eden's and Anitra's arrests—all while situating me at the center of "the whole tangled web of this conspiracy," in his words. The wildly distorted picture Koshy painted of me was of a ruthless opportunist who deliberately duped her friends and family into moving drugs. "Eden was recruited to do this by that defendant right there, Keeda Haynes," he announced, his voice rising almost to a yell as he pointed an accusing finger at me. "Later on, she asked Anitra Haynes, her own *sister*, to be involved in this," he remarked, glaring at the jury in dramatic disbelief. "Ladies and gentlemen, she knew what she was getting into." His insincere smile twisted into a sneer. "She did it for the money," he scoffed, "and for C."

I sat still in my chair, careful not to give Koshy the satisfaction of a reaction, but inside I was screaming. I pressed my frustrations down each time he brought up another deliberate, bold-faced lie.

Then, it was Peter's turn. His statement of the actual facts outlined a very different story—that of a smart young woman with a good head on her shoulders, whose only mistake was falling for the wrong guy. "If they made a movie about Keeda Haynes's involvement in the government's marijuana-by-mail investigation," he said, scanning the faces of the jurors, "it would be called *The Girl Who Knew Too Little and Loved Too Much*." In some ways, the argument Peter laid out was also difficult to hear, but at least it was the truth, even if it was harsh. "I think the proof is going to show that she fell in love with someone that took advantage of her and betrayed her trust," he explained. "And that person was Myron Armstrong."

C. It was C, Peter corrected, who had fed me stories about his nonexistent family business. Who had packages sent to me that were filled with nonexistent beepers and cell phones. It was C who suggested that Eden accept packages—to help her out, he'd said—during that weekend in Memphis, in May of 1999. It was C who reassured me, again and again, that he would never do anything to compromise my life, my future, my family. And it was C who convinced me to believe him. "You are going to have to ask yourselves the hard question," Peter said, addressing the jury, then gesturing toward Sunny Koshy and the rest of the prosecution. "Have they proven, beyond a reasonable doubt, that this girl knew."

The next few days of the trial were a whirlwind of charts and graphs and witness testimonies that included appearances by Eden and Christana; Anitra and my mother; past supervisors from my various retail jobs; Nate and Larry, Marcus and Travis; and, of course, C. Throughout all of it, none of the people knowingly or unknowingly involved in the conspiracy said that I knew what was really inside those boxes. And C himself admitted that he'd always hidden the truth from me. "That's my excuse I used, my lie I told her," he told Sunny Koshy when talking about the fake beepers and pagers business he used to persuade me into accepting the packages. "I was just making it up as I was going." When Koshy pressed him further, trying to ask C—in a million different condescending, demeaning ways—about what he'd *really* told me, what I *really* knew, C finally told him plainly: "I had to not tell her, so we can cover it up so she would be willing to do it. . . . We didn't never tell her that, 'Hey, it's marijuana in these boxes.'"

Much later, after the dust from the trial had settled, C would write me a letter from prison, telling me that Koshy had refused to reduce his twenty-year sentence because he had so severely damaged his case against me. He thought, I supposed, that passing on this bit of information would show that we were on the same team after all; that Sunny Koshy was our common enemy. But reading his words did nothing but confirm for me that I didn't care about his gestures or his intentions. Not anymore. I hadn't cared for a long time.

———

AFTER THREE LONG DAYS OF WITNESS TESTIMONY, IT WAS FINALLY MY turn to take the stand, and I was eager to defend myself. Peter examined me first. It was a small relief—at least I would be starting with a friendly face, with someone who was on my side. He began by leading me through a series of getting-to-know-you questions for the jury, letting my answers build the picture of who I was. He asked about my family and where I had grown up; when I graduated from high school and what I was currently studying in college at TSU. He asked me about my grades—"I'm on the Dean's List," I said—and when I was expected to graduate. It would be in December of 2002, I told him—just seven short months from that day's date. "And what are your plans after you graduate from TSU?" Peter asked me. "To hopefully go to law school." I said.

When we got to the parts of my story that involved C, the packages, and everything that came after, Peter merely reinforced much of what C had already confirmed. That—from start to finish—in a multitude of ways, I was deceived.

Sunny Koshy's approach, in contrast, was to try to trip me up with leading questions and deliberately confusing sentences, often switching subjects abruptly, with the hope that this tactic might result in some kind of "gotcha" moment. "You didn't know I had those transcripts, did you?" he asked me at one point, a smug smile on his face, when he began listing the criminal justice and law enforcement classes I had taken after transferring to TSU in 1999. "I mean, it doesn't matter," I told him, unbothered. "If you had asked me, I would have told you what classes I was taking. I don't have anything to hide."

My major would become a big part of the prosecution's "she-should-have-known" argument, which was turning out to be the strongest leg they had to stand on as all of the others began to buckle during witness testimonies. As if someone studying criminal justice—as a *student in college*—would have learned how to recognize the inner workings of a narcotics operation.

Koshy: "Stuff about drug trafficking comes up in those
    courses, right?"

Me: "No, not in Intro to Criminal Justice or Intro to Law
    Enforcement; no, it didn't."

Koshy: "Don't hear anything about drugs at all?"

Me: "No, it does not. It talks about the formation of the legal
    system, and stuff like that."

Koshy: "Well, you are kind of familiar with drug stuff any-
    way, right? Just from reading the newspaper, things
    like that?"

Me: "Excuse me?"

And so it went, back and forth in this bizarre, infuriating way: Sunny Koshy trying to derail the truth with ridiculous logic, and me trying my best to course-correct his foolishness with the facts.

Memory was also a tactic the prosecution liked to use—asking about very specific activities on very specific dates, three or four years into the past. Details that I could have never known, all this time later, that I would need to hold onto. I didn't know where I had gone with C on, say, Tuesday the 27th of September, 1999, at 2 o'clock p.m., or what we talked about when we got there. The everyday activities that fill up our lives don't stick in our brains that way—it's not how we work, as people. And yet, forgetting, not remembering, misremembering—even pausing too long before responding—these simple realities of being human were miscon- strued as signs of not telling the truth. In this way, even your own memory could be twisted and used against you.

When we finally got to closing arguments on the last day of the trial, I was done—feeling absolutely spent by the whole process. Af- ter days of what seemed like endless rounds of arguments volleyed from one side to the other, as the jury reentered after one last recess, both teams prepared to say their final piece. Addressing them directly, Sunny Koshy laid out more of the same, warping the truth to fit his skewed narrative—that I "received boxes upon boxes of marijuana"; that I "recruited" Eden and later Anitra, my "own flesh and blood," to receive those boxes. And that the entire testimony I gave about not knowing what was really going on didn't "make a wit of common sense." He rolled his eyes and raised his voice and huffed and puffed—punctuating his stories with the dramatic, excessive theatrics he needed to get his lies across.

But the crescendo of Koshy's argument came toward the very end, when he stood facing the jury—the self-righteousness dripping from his words—and told them that my involvement in the conspiracy ultimately came down to one thing: "Her willingness to sell herself [for] $50." The amount of money C had offered me for the trouble of receiving the boxes.

When most of the prosecution's arguments were poked through with holes, Sunny Koshy, as a last resort, equated me with a prostitute. Someone, in this case, willing to engage in illegal activity for a fee.

"There's an old story," he explained, spinning one final image to leave the jury with. "About a well-to-do gentleman, if you want to call him that, approaching a young lady and saying, 'Hey, if I gave you $100,000, would you be intimate with me?' And she says, 'Oh, $100,000? Yeah, okay.' And then the gentleman says, 'Well, I have only got $10 on me, how about for $10?' And she says, 'Hey—what do you think I am?' And the gentleman says, 'Well, we have established what you are. We are just negotiating the price.'"

I couldn't believe what I was hearing. And my female judge—someone we'll soon meet in more detail—sat quietly on her bench, without uttering a single word.

CHAPTER 9

Peter immediately came to my defense in his own closing argument, picking apart the prosecution's assertions about my involvement, claim by claim. That at no point did I ever misinform the investigators, whenever I was asked, or demonstrate some sense of covering up what I "really" knew. That it was C who recruited my loved ones, just as he had recruited me. That not a single one of those who testified could say that I knew about the drugs.

And that, because of these essential truths, in the absence of any concrete evidence proving I knew what had actually gone on, the government had resorted to building its entire case on twisted logic and innuendo to support the story it wanted so badly to hold onto. One that was now based on the assumption that, well, if I didn't know about the drug operation, then I should have. And if I truly did not know, at the very least, I was being deliberately ignorant. This way, even in my innocence, the prosecution could attempt to label me with some form of guilt. And then, it could ask the jury to consider this lack of knowledge when they were coming up with a verdict.

It was a phenomenon that had many names in the legal system—deliberate ignorance, deliberate indifference, willful blindness, conscious avoidance—and it was often used by the prosecution during trials to regain a foothold in its cases when its evidence was otherwise weak. The practice of this kind of doctrine has been called "deeply troubling" by the National Association of Criminal Defense Lawyers, which has been working for years to reform its use in the criminal justice system.

"Deliberate ignorance," Peter argued during the trial, was the Catholic Church turning a blind eye to sexually abusive priests, despite the abundant evidence showing that they had always known what was going on within their walls. "It's not the negligence of a nineteen-year-old girl." A nineteen-year-old girl who, in Peter's words, the government had "the audacity" of calling a whore. "You are going to have to ask yourselves," he paused in front of the jury, "is she really the jezebel that the government is portraying for you, the scheming, sophisticated, shameless, self-promoter; or is she that nineteen-year-old college student, insecure person, that met Myron Armstrong back in 1997 when this all began."

During the course of these last few days, a US attorney, Sunny Koshy, a man who'd been responsible for the intimidation I had experienced for the better part of two years, had characterized me—a then nineteen-year-old African American girl—as a vile, nasty, indecent criminal. Someone willing to sell herself for a price. Me, someone who had never touched a drug or had even a parking ticket to her name. And he did this openly, in court, with the complicit silence of my woman judge. He wove it into the fabric of his argument, using it to support his deeply prejudiced notion that my innocence could never be plausible.

Too often for Black girls, our awareness of the "real" world—including knowing the sinister, the illegal, the uglier parts of it—is assumed as a given by society. For teenage girls who look like me, we've long been painted as sexually advanced and morally corrupt, as jezebels and whores. This idea of Black women and girls as inherently predatory and manipulative goes all the way back to the days of slavery. It was used to uphold white women's purity and to justify our habitual rape by white men. It's the legacy of this old, dangerous stereotype that showed up in the courtroom that day during my trial—coming out of the mouth of a man who represented the US government. And it wouldn't be the last time that this kind of prejudice would rear its ugly head during the process of my case.

CHAPTER 9

"*She* decided to sell herself and make herself a felon," Koshy shot back in his rebuttal to Peter's closing. "All we await is this jury calling her exactly what she is."

Caught between two wildly different portrayals—one comprising truth, the other constructed entirely with bigotry and hate—I waited for the jury to deliver my fate.

chapter 10

I N THE END, AFTER FIVE AND A HALF HOURS OF DELIBERATION, THEY did. Peter would tell me later that as the jurors were filing back to their seats to read the verdict, he thought he saw a few of them discretely smiling our way; they believed, I think, that they would be doing well by us with their decision.

They acquitted me of all of the counts I had been charged with. All except for one: aiding and abetting a conspiracy involving more than one hundred kilograms of marijuana, on the basis of deliberate ignorance. This meant, essentially, that the jury had determined that while I wasn't a knowing member of the drug conspiracy, my involvement helped make it possible. And that I *should* have been aware of what C had gotten me into even if, in truth, I did not.

Koshy's deliberate ignorance tactic had worked. But he and his team still looked shocked when the jury delivered their decision. From across the courtroom, I heard a burst of commotion—audible reactions—from their side. I felt his eyes boring into the back of my head and turned to see him sinking into his chair, glowering in my direction. After the show he had put on over the last week, he was clearly upset that his takedown didn't go entirely his way.

Even so, the prosecution's damage was very much done. On top of its successful deliberate ignorance argument, I had been convicted for the *total* amount of marijuana that was determined to have circulated throughout the entirety of the conspiracy by all of its handlers—including during the time well before I had even met C. Because of this crucial factor in the conviction—"more than 100 kilograms"—that single aiding and abetting charge carried the same weight as the others would have, had the jury determined that I knowingly committed those crimes. Because of the mandate of the federal mandatory minimum sentencing guidelines, my punishment would be just as harsh.

I would be facing *no less* than sixty months in prison or five years.

Mandatory minimum sentencing laws, which require judges to hand down automatic minimum prison sentences for certain offenses, particularly drug-related ones, had been ravaging American communities for decades. In the early 1970s, then-president Richard Nixon officially declared a "War on Drugs," beginning a slew of strict federal policies created to start lengthening drug sentences and to expand government agencies responsible for drug control. In the 1980s, President Reagan took the War on Drugs to the next level, resulting in the historic 1984 Comprehensive Crime Control Act, which officially established mandatory minimum sentencing. Although devised to catch those at the top of the drug trade and deter others from entering, in reality these policies threw hundreds of thousands of low-level, nonviolent, often first-time offenders into the prison system for years—ruining lives and breaking up families.

In the period that followed, more federal mandatory minimum sentencing policies were enacted, triggering minimum sentences for possession of certain drugs. This would essentially criminalize drug possession along racial and economic lines. For instance, distribution of five grams of crack cocaine—a drug that had started decimating predominately low-income Black and brown communities during the 1980s—carried the same five-year minimum sentence as distribution of five hundred grams of powder cocaine, a much more expensive alternative that was found more often in affluent white communities. It was a ratio of one hundred to one, based on the erroneous, racism-laced belief that crack cocaine was more dangerous than powder. According to the American Civil Liberties Union (ACLU), in 1986, before these mandatory minimum sentencing laws for crack cocaine offenses were implemented, the average federal drug sentence for African Americans was 11 percent higher than for whites. Four years later, the average federal drug sentence for African Americans was 49 percent higher.

Since the War on Drugs began, the number of people incarcerated for drug offenses in the United States catapulted from a little over forty thousand in 1980, to well over four hundred thousand in 2019. In 2002, the year of my trial, that number was steadily climbing. And I was soon to be another number added to the statistics.

It was a blow. A lifetime of believing in the power of truth and innocence as an ultimately exonerating force had all come down to this.

We would appeal, of course. But we couldn't do that until after the conclusion of my sentencing hearing, which wasn't scheduled for another four months. The judge and the prosecution were prepared to send me back to jail right then and there, immediately after the trial proceedings were over. They began looking through the sentencing guidelines, trying to find the language that justified putting me away immediately. Tracing a finger over a page, Judge Aleta Trauger read: "'A person who has been found guilty of an offense that carries a maximum term of imprisonment under the Controlled

Substances Act of ten years or more'—and this one does—'and is awaiting imposition or execution of a sentence [must] be detained unless judicial officer finds there's substantial likelihood that a motion for acquittal or new trial will be granted, or an attorney for the government has recommended that no sentence of imprisonment be imposed on a person'—and I don't believe you could make that recommendation in this case."

"I would direct the Court's attention to the statutory language, the text of (f) (1) (C)," Peter chimed in. Quick on his feet with a counterargument, Peter had been reading over the same guidelines Koshy and Judge Trauger had been reviewing and found a critical hole in their interpretations. While there are some statutes that say if you are found guilty of certain crimes you must be detained immediately, my charge was not one of them. The judge and Koshy had been basing their argument for immediate detainment on the wrong section of the guidelines—the one under the crimes that I had been charged with but ultimately acquitted of. "This jury has found her guilty of 18 U.S.C. 2," Peter corrected. "So by the plain reading of the text of the statute, it doesn't apply." The judge had no choice but to concede.

"Yeah, it doesn't apply," she said, rereading the language once again. "I agree with you."

By the Grace of God—and the brilliance of Peter—I was allowed to stay in the custody of my parents and continue going to work and school while we awaited my next round of judgment: the sentencing hearing.

———

AFTER A WEEK OF INTENSITY IN THE COURTROOM, I WAS ABSOLUTELY exhausted. The night it was over, as I was lying in bed preparing to go to sleep, Pinky came into my room to check on how I was doing. She sat on the edge of my bed, talking to me about the past few days. Before she got up to leave, she bent down to kiss my forehead. "Everything is going be alright, Ke-Ke," she said, calling me by the nickname that only she was allowed to call me. Pinky had affectionately referred to me as her "Ke-Ke" since I was a little kid. For as long as I could remember, my grandmother had been the person in my family who understood me most. If you asked any of the grandkids who Pinky's favorite was, we'd each be convinced that it was us. That's just the type of person she was. She made each and every one of us feel special—wholly and individually seen.

In that moment, when she told me everything was going to be all right, I knew that my grandmother wasn't trying to wave a magic wand and make everything better. We both knew that the situation was what it was, and no amount of nice words could change that reality. But she also believed in me; Pinky knew that I would continue to do whatever I needed to do in order to be okay. To keep meeting the goals I set for myself. Things would be all right, eventually. Somehow. I prayed that God would find a way. *I just have to keep pushing,* I told myself, thinking about the fact that—amidst all of this—I would soon be approaching my last semester at TSU.

Keep moving, I thought. *The only thing I can do is control what I can control.*

I was going to tackle the last half of my senior year with a laser sharp focus—putting up blinders as best as I could; blocking out anything that could derail me if I let it. And there was plenty to be distracted by if I was a different kind of person. In the wake of the trial, the small-town gossip machine around Franklin immediately got to work, spreading misinformation about me and my case. I even heard that one girl in town asked my cousin what I was going to do with my clothes when I went to prison; apparently she wanted first dibs.

Not all of the rumors got back to me, but even if they did, it wouldn't have made much difference. This kind of chatter was unnecessary noise. No one who loved me doubted who I was, or distanced themselves, or judged; those who doubted me knew nothing about what had really happened, anyway. They were not there for any of the events that had occurred during these last few years; they did not know the actual details of my case. So why would I care about what they said? I have always been defiant that way.

Keep moving. Keep pushing. There were more important things at stake.

My sentencing hearing was scheduled for later that fall, and in the months in between I had to meet with another court official, this time an icy, blue-eyed presentencing officer named Lori Pridgen. Her job was to go through the records of my case to help the judge come to a decision about the length of my sentence. While, in theory, the presentencing officer is supposed to be an objective fact finder, compiling her own report of recommendations for the judge by using both sides' information, in my case, Pridgen used only one version: the prosecution's. She came into our first meeting with her mind very much made up about my guilt.

Sitting down with her and Peter, it felt like even her most innocuous questions—Where do you work? Do you have any assets?—were dripping with accusations. At one point, during a particularly brutal, condescending round of questioning, in an effort to keep me calm, Peter discretely reached out and touched the side of my leg. We both knew that this woman's treatment was wrong, and Peter sensed that I had reached the limit of what I could endure. Maya Angelou once said that people will forget what you said or did, but they will never forget how you made them feel. Lori Pridgen's exact words are now lost to me so many years later, but the sting of them burns whenever I recall our meeting that day. I felt small and dehumanized, judged as "less than" under her intense scrutiny.

When the report was typed and finished, she had characterized me as being a primary manager, organizer, and leader of the entire drug conspiracy. Pridgen felt that I should get an *enhancement* in my sentencing because of this role and that I should not be granted leniency of any kind, since I had elected to go to trial.

Pause and think about this: we have a constitutional right to a fair and public trial under the Sixth Amendment, and yet people are routinely punished by the government for exercising it. Statistics show that defendants who have been convicted of drug offenses with mandatory minimum sentences who went to trial, like me, receive sentences on average eleven years *longer* than those who plead guilty. Among first-time offenders facing mandatory minimum drug sentences, those who go to trial receive almost twice the sentence length of those who plead guilty. I couldn't blame my codefendants for not wanting to go to trial; their punishments would have undoubtedly been harsher if they had. The risk of taking advantage of a right they were entitled to was just too high. For Black people especially, the task of weighing the risks when it comes to pushing for what we are entitled to is all too familiar.

What kind of justice system is this?

Lori Pridgen's concluding recommendation was that I spend 108 to 135 months in prison—or a maximum of a little over eleven years. This was six years *over* the mandatory minimum sentence I was already facing. Peter filed an objection to the report, reemphasizing the facts of my case and my accurate telling of events, not the government's erroneous version of it. And while they went back and forth about the report, it was the slanted version that ultimately got into the hands of Judge Trauger during the sentencing hearing that occurred that September.

Keep moving. Keep pushing, I told myself, over and over again. *God will find a way.* In just a few short months, I would graduate. Any future beyond that was out of my hands.

"OH, WE HAVE A LOT OF ISSUES." ON THE MORNING OF THE SENTENC-
ing hearing, Judge Trauger looked through the existing presentencing report, seeing all the places where Peter had noted our objections.
Sunny Koshy and his team sat at a table across the aisle from ours,
ready to take one last shot at burying me—as deep as they could—
beneath any legal statutes they could use to their advantage. Now
corroborated by the skewed presentencing report, Koshy pushed for
me to get more time for my role of "conducting sales and recruit-
ment meetings" with my friends and sister, and allegedly, according
to him, acting as C's right hand.

Thankfully, Judge Trauger didn't go for it. Based on the evidence
Peter had argued and her own notes from my trial—over which
she had also presided—she determined that I ultimately had no
decision-making authority and therefore couldn't have been the
mastermind Koshy had painted me to be. Any proposed additions
to my sentence on that basis would be removed.

It seemed, at least during these beginning moments, that there
might be some hope in the wreckage of this ordeal. In 1998, Aleta
Trauger was appointed by then-president Bill Clinton as the first female US district judge for the Middle District of Tennessee, and since
then she had garnered a reputation for being a lenient sentencer. But
as the hearing wore on, it was clear that any favor she had for us—
for me—had been spent. After this moment, it was all downhill.

Every subsequent point Peter made that might give the judge a
pathway to leniency was minimized or dismissed. She rejected the
argument that I could have been so thoroughly manipulated by C.
She countered instead that a smart girl like me, someone who came
from a stable family, who had demonstrated such strength and assertiveness in the courtroom, could only have been willfully ignorant
in this situation. The she-should-have-known argument came back to bite
me once again. "The notion that somehow he was keeping her so

involved, that she just had no will of her own, the Court doesn't find that flies."

Regardless of the objections we had made to the presentencing report, regardless of Peter's arguments during the hearing, Judge Trauger was willing to accept the government's version as fact. She had made up her mind.

It's true that Sonny Koshy had a narrative that he was pushing all this time—bending the facts, however he could, to fit his story of Keeda Haynes, the manipulative drug kingpin. But Judge Trauger had a narrative too. If I had come from a "broken" home or had a history of drugs, or maybe if I hadn't graduated from high school or gone to college, then my actions might have been justified and deserving of her leniency. *Well, there you go,* she might say. *Unfortunate girl with an unfortunate past caught up with the wrong guy.* But because the details of my life didn't add up to the conclusion she wanted to make, she would punish me for diverging from her script. If it didn't make sense to her, then it must not make sense objectively. It had to be wrong. There was a blind spot her logic didn't account for—one that too many judges in her position had: the reality of the criminal justice system itself. That Black and brown people don't have to be guilty of something—whatever that something is—to be brought into the system. That the fact of our Blackness, or our brownness, is often reason enough.

The mandatory minimum of my sentence was sixty months, or five years. With some additional points the prosecution had successfully argued for my role in the operation—largely based on my proximity to C, as his girlfriend—I was looking at a range of seventy-eight to ninety-seven months. Between six and a half to eight years.

"Now, in terms of where I sentence the defendant within that range, Mr. Strianse, I'm ready to hear from you," Judge Trauger said, glancing up from her papers. She then shifted her glance, looking now at me. "Ms. Haynes, I'd like to hear from you, and we'll go from there. You have a right to be heard. I hope that you will talk to me. You don't have to."

It was a strange scene. The judge was telling Peter and me that she did not believe us, and that no arguments or evidence we might offer could change her mind. She had definitively laid the gavel down on my freedom—I would be without it for at least the next six and a half years. But she was also saying that she wanted to hear from me before she determined just how much of it she would take away. The request was framed as a courtesy: "You have a right to be heard," she had said. But in reality, it felt like a condescending taunt. A tap dance for my liberty; a test to see how much I would grovel for any lingering scrap of grace she might be willing to toss my way.

Peter and I hadn't prepared for me to speak, so we asked for a recess to regroup. It was clear to both of us that there was nothing we could do to get through to her. But we talked through a plan of what I would say to Judge Trauger anyway, hoping against hope that it might help us.

When we returned to the courtroom an hour later, I was ready to speak my piece. My parents both sat quietly in the back of the courtroom, in silent support.

"First of all, I would like to say—this is hard," I broke off, gathering myself up. I took a breath and started over:

"I'm sorry to my family for everything I have put them through. I'm sorry that you had to sit through this. I'm sorry that I had to be here. I'm not a bad person. If I had known that it was drugs that was in those boxes, I wouldn't have never accepted those boxes in a million years. I have never done anything wrong in my life. Never.

"And I would have never accepted those boxes if I had known that it was drugs in it. Even after Eden, I would have put my life on the line saying that it was still cell phones and pagers in those boxes.

I mean, I just—I would have never accepted those boxes if I had known there was drugs in there.

"I wouldn't have put my family through that. I would not have risked everything that I have worked so hard to accomplish. I am three months from graduating from school. I have worked so hard to get here. And I would have never, ever jeopardized that in a million years, not for nothing.

"I just—I just wish that I could close my eyes and all this would go away. I wish it had never happened. I mean, the only thing I did wrong was to love him and trust him with my heart. That was the biggest mistake that I could have ever made in my life, and I'm sorry."

I sat back down in my seat, glad that at least that part was over. Peter stood up next, tossing one last Hail Mary to Judge Trauger—asking if she would consider, at least, sentencing me at the lowest end of the range she had decided on: seventy-eight months. "What I have been struck by in knowing Ms. Haynes is her courage," Peter said, placing a hand on my shoulder. "It took great courage to take this case to trial. She knew what the potential downside would be. And it's going to take even greater courage for her to go and do this sentence, and do it with the right attitude where she could come out and continue to be productive. . . . She was well on her way to making something of herself before this whole unfortunate incident unfolded."

We had done all we could.

After listening quietly to our pleas, her face giving nothing away, Judge Trauger rifled through her notes, then finally opened her mouth to speak. "It's hard to give Ms. Haynes the bottom of the guideline because the Court is not impressed with her attitude today. I think she is continuing to lie to herself."

There it was. Clearly, I hadn't complied with the story the judge wanted me to tell. "To the Court, the proof was overwhelming that she either remained deliberately ignorant, or didn't remain deliberate and was just kidding herself," Judge Trauger continued. There was no way, she seemed to think, that I could not have known. She thought I was "very lucky," in fact, to have been acquitted of the charges I was acquitted of.

"So despite the fact that 78 months should be enough for a first-time offender," Judge Trauger concluded, "I can't give her 78 months. I'm going to give her 84 months, 7 years."

Despite the mountain of facts that proved what I did not know, Judge Trauger, like the prosecution itself, preferred instead to base her decision on an assumption—on, ultimately, a judgment of my character. That regardless of the evidence before us, someone who looked like me simply should have known.

I was floored. Nothing about this logic made any kind of sense.

But, I know now, presumptions like these make the criminal justice system go 'round. They are the reason African Americans are imprisoned at almost six times the rate of whites; why people of color are disproportionately populating our prisons; why Black people represent 47 percent of those who have been exonerated for being wrongfully accused. It's why federal prosecutors, like Sunny Koshy, are twice as likely to charge Black people like me with offenses that carry a mandatory minimum sentence than white people facing similar charges.

And for Black women, we are saddled with an added layer of unique discrimination, based on our gender. There was a name for the kind of judgment I faced during the entirety of my trial. I didn't know it then, but I do now. It's called adultification bias, and it's leveled specifically against Black girls, who are often deemed by adults as less innocent, less deserving of empathy, and more adultlike than white girls of the same age. According to a 2017 report from the Georgetown Law Center on Poverty and Inequality, "Adultification contributes to a false narrative that black youths' transgressions are intentional and malicious, instead of the result of immature decision making—a key characteristic of childhood."

Like so much when it comes to discrimination and prejudice, the foundation of adultification bias is systemic. It's rooted in the same historic bigotry that empowered Sunny Koshy to equate me with a prostitute in the courtroom during my trial and excused Judge Trauger's silence when he did. The same one that allowed him, during my sentencing hearing, to argue that I receive the upper range of my sentence length on the grounds that I demonstrated "extremely bad qualities," especially that I "corrupted" and "sacrificed" my own sister. Or that prompted an entire discussion about my demeanor, my assertiveness construed as a fault. My refusal to back away from the truth was viewed as a mark of aggression. It's the kind of stereotype that Black women are constantly fighting in every single area of our lives: When we choose to stand up for ourselves, we're combative. When we fight for ourselves, for our liberty—even in the criminal justice system—the Angry Black Woman trope still holds.

"The court is not impressed with her attitude today," Judge Trauger had said, before deciding to put me away for seven years.

Studies show that adultification bias is linked to harsher punishment of Black girls, both in the education and criminal justice systems. Black girls are 2.7 times more likely to be referred to the juvenile justice system than their white peers. Black women are incarcerated at a rate two times higher than white women. Clearly, the ramifications of this phenomenon were evident, and they were very, very real. For women who look like me—Black women— we are not just fighting against the criminal justice system. We are fighting against the racism and sexism that have been deeply ingrained into our society—in all of its functions, in infinite ways— for centuries.

And so, it was decided. Judge Trauger announced that after I finished my studies at TSU that December, I would report to the Alderson Federal Women's Prison Camp in West Virginia, to begin a seven-year sentence for a crime I did not commit. All because I should have known.

We would push for acquittal, making the deliberate ignorance instruction—the she-should-have-known argument—one of our centerpiece objections.

———

I GRADUATED FROM TSU ON DECEMBER 17, 2002, WITH A DEGREE IN criminal justice, minoring in psychology. I had finished with honors, on the Dean's List—having not missed a single assignment, not a single paper, during the entire course of this ordeal. I had completed this important step, even as all the next ones in my future felt out of view. The festivities to celebrate this accomplishment with family were all overshadowed by that unknown; by the creeping possibility that, at any moment, the bridge I was building for the next stage of my life would disappear. I'm not going to prison, I continued to repeat to myself.

Right after the sentencing, we began the process of filing the motion for my appeal, putting every bit of our hope and belief in its success. Additionally, Peter filed another motion requesting that I stay out on bond while the appeal was pending, which would allow me to avoid reporting to prison while my actual appeal was going through the process of being approved or denied.

Fully believing that our request would be approved, during my last semester at school I applied for a legal secretary position at a law firm in Nashville. It would be my first significant step forward in realizing my next goal of becoming a lawyer. I submitted my résumé, completed my rounds of interviews, and waited—determined to continue living my life, to not allow this conviction to prevent me from moving forward.

A few weeks later, I got the job. I accepted the position, excited by the possibility that my life could carry on as it had before all this started. But as the weeks wore on, my appeal for bond continued to hang in the balance.

And then, the worst-case scenario materialized: two weeks before I was scheduled to report to Alderson Federal Women's Prison Camp, my request to stay out of custody while Peter and I appealed my case was denied.

I was numb. I felt that bridge I was building for my future begin to crumble beneath me.

chapter 11

O N JANUARY 6, 2003, ON THE VERY SAME DAY MY NEW JOB should have started, I would be reporting, instead, to federal prison.

We left for Alderson on a Sunday. Because I had to report early the next day, the plan was to leave in the afternoon and drive through the night to get to the compound in West Virginia that Monday morning. I began that last day in Franklin like so many I'd had before. I got up and dressed, then took the one-minute walk down Granbury Street, toward Natchez, to go to Providence—the same church I'd attended all my life. I joined my family inside, and we sat in our regular spots in the last rows of the pews, listening to the deacons' opening hymns, the choir's songs, the pastor's sermon.

Like so many Sundays before, after church we made the short walk back to Sue Lee's house to gather. Aunts and uncles, cousins and family friends came in and out of the house to visit as they normally did. Except this time, in addition to the usual communing, I would have to say my goodbyes. And this time, unlike so many times before, Sue Lee wouldn't be there.

My great-grandmother's colon cancer had returned, and in the time leading up to my departure to Alderson, she had started to seriously decline. Sue Lee had been in the hospital for at least a week or so before I left—the ravages of the cancer slowly starting to take effect on her body and on her mind. The chemo had taken all of her hair and turned her once light-brown skin grey. Lying in her hospital bed, she was in and out of consciousness; in and out of recognizing the small circle of family members and friends who were allowed to go in and visit her. It was hard on all of us to picture her this way— the strong, vibrant matriarch of our family, reduced to a shell of herself. Many of us chose not to go see her in the hospital, including me. I didn't want to leave home with an image of what the cancer had done to her. I couldn't let myself remember her like that. So I held onto the memories I had of her instead: of Sue Lee sitting in her favorite chair on the porch; of my afternoons watching her make cha-cha pickles; of the years she spent loving all of us as the anchor of our family.

With only a little time left before we needed to go, I walked back to my house to change out of my church clothes and to gather up the few personal items I knew I could take with me. Having only found out a couple of weeks before that our motion to stay out on bond pending appeal was denied, my things weren't packed up at all—I didn't think I would be going to prison, and even when that reality did become clear, I didn't think I could possibly be staying long.

I went to my room to retrieve my glasses, unsure about whether they would let me keep my contacts. Then, I picked up the black leather Bible my dad had given me a few years before. It would be coming with me too. After that, I found a scrap of paper and began writing down the phone numbers of the people I wanted to reach most: my parents; my sister, Anitra; Pinky; my aunts; and a couple of friends. By then, I knew Peter's contact information by heart; I didn't need to write it down. I looked over the list again, double-checking names and numbers, then slipped it between the pages of my Bible.

Then I stepped back out through my bedroom one last time, closing the door behind me.

The drive to Alderson was long—eight to ten hours depending on your route. Though my parents had gotten divorced by then, they were both in the car for the ride. Winding through Kentucky and Virginia, the three of us drove through the blue-grey landscape, snow powdering the roads as we inched closer to West Virginia. It was a quiet trip. Looking out of the window, I watched it all go by, then eventually drifted off to sleep as afternoon turned into evening. Hour after hour passed, as we drove through the mountains in the dark. Then, eventually, we turned onto a smooth paved road lined with thick trees. We stopped the car in front of a black iron gate held in place by a massive cobblestoned wall. I would have thought that we had pulled up to the entrance of some fancy gated community, were it not for the bronze plaque inlaid on the left side of the wall that read: "Federal Industrial Institution for Women." At the other end of the wall stood another sign that gave a more specific description of where we were:

U.S. Department of Justice

Bureau of Prisons

F. P. C. ALDERSON, W.V.

AUTHORIZED TRAFFIC ONLY

It was the middle of the night and pitch-black outside; our headlights illuminating just enough to see the gate and the stone wall and the fence—and to make shadows of the trees surrounding us. I got out of the car and walked to the intercom near the gate, pressing a button to announce that I had arrived. "Hello? This is Keeda Haynes," I said, speaking into the little black box to whomever was listening.

"I'm here to turn myself in." A few moments passed before a crackly voice on the other end replied: "Someone's coming out to get you."

Within five minutes or so, a white pickup truck bearing the Federal Bureau of Prisons seal began driving toward us, slowing to a stop on the inside of the gate. It was time for me to go inside. I collected my things from the car—holding onto my Bible, my list of phone numbers, my glasses—and hugged my parents goodbye, not knowing when I might see them again.

I was alone in the truck, save for the officers who were driving. We rode in silence, the darkness hiding the landscape around us. After a few minutes, we arrived in front of the administration building, a two-story, old-fashioned brick structure that housed the Receiving & Discharge (R&D) Department, where I was placed in a cell with two other women who had also just come in and were waiting to be processed. Alderson operates on a standard Monday through Friday, 8 a.m. to 4 p.m., schedule—which meant that because we arrived in the middle of the night, the compound was closed. It would be hours before anyone from R&D was scheduled to be there, leaving the three of us new arrivals—called "new commits"—to wait together until someone came to process us in. I don't remember much of any conversation between us during this time, but I did learn their names: Christy and Elizabeth. Christy, I would never really talk to again, but Elizabeth, a white girl around my age with glasses, from North Carolina, would eventually become a close friend.

Finally, the officers from R&D unlocked our cell a little after 8 a.m. and began processing us into the facility one by one: First Christy, then Elizabeth, then finally me. After being fingerprinted and photographed, I was told to go into the bathroom to remove all my clothes, then place them into a bag that would be mailed back to my parents in Tennessee. I returned to the room naked, where I was instructed to lift my chest, then to squat and cough, while the officers scrutinized my every movement, staring with hardened eyes. The strip search was humiliating. It was just one of the many things you were made to endure as the system attempted to transform you from human being to inmate. An ID card was made with the photograph they'd taken of me and attached to a lanyard, which I was told to wear around my neck at all times. Looking at the card, an unsmiling girl stared back at me, "00017-011" printed underneath. The number that would follow me from this moment forward.

Dressed again in an orange jumpsuit they gave us to walk through the compound, the officers pointed to the backdoor of the building and told me to proceed to Laundry, where I would get all the basic necessities to start my new life at Alderson: sheets and towels and toiletries, along with what they called "newbie clothes." They asked me for my size, and I went to a small dressing room to begin trying on what would become my uniform from now on: khaki pants and tops and brown T-shirts when the weather got warmer.

Once my size was sorted, the staff gave me more changes of clothes to stuff in my mesh laundry bag, along with prison-issued underwear and socks; two towels and washcloths; some deodorant, toothpaste, and shampoo; a stiff cotton blanket; and a couple of white flat sheets. I left the dressing room in my newbie clothes, putting on the oversized coat and steel-toed shoes they had handed over, then made my way across the compound to find the unit where I would be living.

Stepping outside from Laundry for the first time in the light of day, I started to take in my surroundings. First of all, the space was *enormous*—Alderson was a compound in the truest sense of the word. The prison camp was situated on over a hundred acres of sloping land, with the silhouette of the Blue Ridge Mountains dotting the background. With no fences or armed officers guarding the property, the mountains and natural isolation were thought to be sufficient barriers to deter escape for the over one thousand women who were imprisoned here. Sidewalks connected each building to the next, and a hill running through the center divided the prison camp into upper and lower parts—the top and the bottom of the compound.

At the bottom of the hill, next to the Laundry and R&D buildings, were also some of the sixteen original cottages that comprised the prison when Alderson opened in 1927. It was the first federal prison built specifically for women, known over the years to house political agitators and government spies, would-be assassins and the wives of mobsters. Alderson had even received its share of celebrities, like the iconic jazz singer Billie Holiday, there for possession of narcotics—hounded by the federal government in the 1940s and 1950s, during the very beginnings of America's War on Drugs. Or probably its most famous resident to-date: Martha Stewart.

The picturesque compound was modeled after the campus of Bucknell University in Pennsylvania, designed to invoke a sense of intimacy and freedom and "home." But walking through Alderson in the cold, wearing my drab government-issued prison uniform, weighed down by my steel-toed shoes and the heavy laundry bag slung across my back—filled with more government-issued things that were not mine—there was no confusing this "nice" place for home; there was no thinking of this environment with a sense of freedom.

My housing unit was located in an area at the top of the compound called "The Range," where most of the new people resided when they were first processed. There were no tour guides assigned while I tried to navigate my way there, no guards on hand showing the way. Like everything in prison, you simply had to figure it out. New commits at Alderson were easy to spot, between the orange jumpsuits or newbie clothes, the huge laundry bag being dragged along beside them, and often the look of confusion on their faces.

But I quickly discovered that the other women in the compound were more than willing to point you in whatever direction you needed to go. With the help of a passing group, I eventually got my bearings and began the long trek uphill to reach my unit inside Range 3.

I continued to go through the motions for the rest of the day: checking in with the CO at the officer station near the entrance of the unit who'd been alerted to my arrival, waiting for them to assign me to a bunk. Walking past a cluster of five or six freestanding bunks near the officer station I learned was called the "bus stop," I was escorted to the area in Range 3, where I would now be spending so much of my time. I put my stuff on the top bunk I was told was mine and scanned the room around me. Each range held about 120 women in a big, open space divided into rows of concrete, door-less cubicles—called "cubes." Each row of cubes faced the next one, with about thirty cubes in a row. Inside each one was space enough for one set of bunk beds, two metal lockers for you and your room-mate to store your clothes, a single desk, and a trash can. This was my new home.

I turned back to my bunk to begin making my bed, but two women in my unit who happened to be walking by called me to lunch in-stead. At Alderson, I would learn, all activities revolved around a strict schedule, and we had to be at the Central Dining Room (CDR) and back to our respective cubes before the lunch hour was over. "You can walk down with us," Tanesha and Valerie told me. I knew they were just being nice, seeing that I was clearly new and alone—I was the only one making my bed in the middle of the day as everyone else was at work. Still, I genuinely appreciated the gesture. We walked out of the Range, passing the recreational building—which held the gym, the library, and the chapel—before heading down a dirt hill to the bottom of the compound, where CDR was located. It was easy to see why so many of the women traded in their steel-toed boots for tennis shoes if they could afford the $70 to buy them at the commissary—walking up and down these hills and across this huge campus, I could feel my feet aching even after that one day.

By the time we got back to the Range after lunch, I was exhausted. I felt like I'd lived a whole week in these last twelve hours. Finally with nowhere to be and no one to report to, I made my bed quickly and fell into a tired sleep. But after what seemed like only seconds, I was called awake again by one of the guards. "Report to R&D," he told me. "The lieutenant wants to see you." *The lieutenant?* I had no idea what he could possibly want from me. I had been at Alderson for barely a day.

When I walked into the lieutenant's office, the presentencing report from my trial was sitting on top of his desk. "I want to talk about your time as a correctional officer," he said, eyeing the section of the report that went over my employment history. How long was I a CO for? he wanted to know. What kind of training did I go through? Which codes did we use in the jails? He asked these questions conversationally at first, before drilling deeper and deeper down for more details. Mining to see what exactly I remembered, which, admittedly, was not that much. It had been at least two or three years at that point since I last worked in the jails.

Still, the lieutenant proceeded to grill me for the next forty-five minutes, moving from my time as a CO to the topic of my criminal justice degree and my psychology minor. What kinds of classes was I taught? he asked me. What was my understanding of the criminal justice system? he dug a little more. "And did I read in here that you went to law school?" He looked up from my report again, turning the pages casually, keeping his tone even. "No," I responded. *Not yet.* "It's all there in the report."

"Well, we need to make sure you won't be a breach to security," the lieutenant finally revealed. *A breach to what?* Apparently, the details of my background—having spent some time as a correctional officer myself; having studied the criminal justice system and shown an interest in the law—these were enough to raise alarm bells that I might pose a threat to the security of the facility. With all that knowledge, they thought—who knows—I might stage a coup or try to bust myself or others out. *This is totally ridiculous*, I thought, looking at him from across the desk.

The lieutenant finally said I could go and sent me back to my unit. But it wouldn't be the first time they would eye me cautiously, presuming that my knowledge was a threat to their control.

————

MY INITIAL DAYS AT ALDERSON ALL BLEND TOGETHER IN MY MIND. There were medical exams and tests and evaluations and some semblance of an orientation that did little to orient me to the new reality I was trying to grasp. I would come to understand that our days revolved around Count Time, which allowed the COs to take stock of where each of the inmates was at any given moment. At designated times throughout the day, a whistle that sounded like it was coming from a freight train rang out from a building called the Powerhouse at the bottom of the hill—loud enough to be heard throughout the entire compound.

Standing counts in the mornings, afternoons, and evenings required every woman to stand near her bunk bed until the count was cleared; and special counts and emergency counts could happen at any time at an officer's discretion, announced by three short blasts of the Powerhouse whistle, usually signaling that someone was missing. Count Times even happened when we were meant to be sleeping—officers swept through the Range during the late-night hours with flashlights, scanning the bunk beds. The rules forbade us from being too covered up by blankets and sheets: "The correctional officers must see human flesh," it read in the handbook we were given. It was not uncommon for the (predominately male) officers to throw the covers off you or lift them up in the middle of the night to check that you were, in fact, there.

After the count cleared in the morning and the compound officially opened, each inmate reported to work—a mandatory requirement at Alderson. Every inmate held a job in some part of the grounds—cleaning the administrative buildings or the dining hall, mowing the huge fields in the landscaping unit, fixing cars in the garage, doing masonry. Earning our "living" for a meager twelve cents an hour. At Alderson, I had become the government's slave.

A couple of days after I arrived, once I passed all my medical exams, they assigned me to work lunch and dinner at Central Dining Room (CDR), the typical first job for new arrivals at the prison camp. Each afternoon before lunch began, I dressed in the white uniform I was given and headed down to the dining hall, where I cleaned off tables and swept and mopped the floors while the thousands of women in the compound streamed in and out. When the shift finally ended, I walked back to the living units with other women I worked with, the smells of CDR still clinging to my uniform. Struggling at the end of each day to wrap my head around the fact that this—all of this—was the life I was now living.

At least, in my unit, I was beginning to make connections with the women around me. Elizabeth, the brown-haired girl with glasses from North Carolina, whom I'd met in R&D, when we were both waiting to be processed, turned out to live in my Range. We formed a close friend group with two other women who also lived in our Range: Terry, a white woman from West Virginia who had arrived at Alderson a few weeks before me, and Allie, a girl about my age whose family moved to Ohio from Ethiopia when she was younger. Allie and I quickly became best friends; she had come to Alderson only about a week before I got there, and we talked a lot about what it was like to adjust to this place, and what our lives were like before we got here. She was big into church as well, and we bonded over our shared spirituality.

One evening, at the end of my first week at Alderson, I remember talking with Allie in her cube after dinner. We were sitting on her top bunk, chatting about where we were and how we got there, and about the sentences we both were facing. She had a year and a day until she was released. I, on the other hand, had seven years.

From the vantage point of Allie's top bunk, we could see the entire Range—over one hundred beds spread out before us, in what seemed like an endless expanse. *Oh my God*, I thought, as I slowly scanned the room, looking from bunk bed to bunk bed, cubicle to cubicle to cubicle. *I'm in fucking federal prison. And I'm going to be here for seven years.*

During this entire ordeal, I could count on one hand the number of times I actually cried. And in this moment, staring out at the Range, knowing that this might be the same view I would see for my next seven birthdays, the next seven years of holidays and missed activities with loved ones—the next seven years of my life—the tears began to fall.

"Keeda, listen—you won't be here for seven years," Allie told me, squeezing my hand. "You're going to win your appeal, and you're going to go home."

I hoped and prayed that she was right. But the road ahead would be impossibly long.

chapter 12

I F MY FIRST WEEK AT ALDERSON COULD BE SUMMED UP AS ACKNOWL-edgment, the second week would be defined by grief.

I was standing next to my bunk bed one afternoon, waiting for the four o'clock count to clear across the compound. Because everyone on the grounds had to be accounted for, the whole process usually took about an hour to complete. But considering this was such a big operation, involving so many people, Count Times were typically quiet. When the COs strolled into your unit, yelling "Count Time!" that was your cue to move quickly inside your cube to be counted. When they passed, there was no talking permitted, no movement, no noise of any kind. All of us stood in our places as the correctional officers walked by wordlessly, glancing at our IDs before marking us down on the clipboards they carried around with them. Once accounted for, you were free to move about your unit once again. They had already been through most of the compound, including my section of the Range, which meant that at any moment the Powerhouse whistle would blow, signaling that we could carry on with the rest of our evening.

But the minutes ticked by, and there was still no whistle. Then, suddenly, an officer emerged at the opposite end of the hallway from where I was standing, walking toward me with Alderson's prison chaplain, Elizabeth Walker. I hadn't met Chaplain Walker personally yet, but I had seen her a few times while I checked out the chapel in the days before. She was middle-aged and white—and loved by most of the women at the camp. People loved to visit her in the chapel, but everybody knew that if you saw Chaplain Walker inside the Range, nine times out of ten she wasn't there to deliver good news.

As she and the officer made their way down the hallway, passing each of the cubes, somehow it got quieter than it already was—the entire Range was hushed, save for the sounds of their shoes clicking against the cement floor. Having been in Alderson for only two weeks at that point, the significance of Chaplain Walker's unexpected appearance was completely lost on me. I had no idea why she and the officer had stopped in front of my bed; why they then told me to come with them. But as I walked back through the silent hallway, the other women knew; their eyes followed me as I passed. Nearly all of them, at one point or another, had been in my place before.

Still accompanied by the officer, Chaplain Walker led me to the officer's station at the front of my unit and gestured for me to sit down. "Your mother called," she said, leaning on the desk beside me. "She told us that your great-grandmother passed away today."

A wave of shock passed through my body. Sue Lee had been in my life for as long as I had been living, and I never imagined what it could possibly be like without her. I was devastated.

My great-grandmother was our family's center. It was with Sue Lee, at the house on Granbury Street, that I spent nearly every day of my childhood. It was to her that I went whenever I was home sick from school, eating hot cornbread and buttermilk that she'd break up in a cup and give to me, measuring the day by the times her favorite soap operas came on. For me, Sue Lee was the person I conjured most when I thought of home. And now she was gone.

I was numb. At some point Chaplain Walker told me that I could go into the chapel and call my family. When my mother answered the phone, she confirmed the news of my great-grandmother's passing. "I talked to Peter too," she added. "He said he's going to try to figure out a way to get you to the funeral."

When I spoke with Peter later that day, he told me that he'd talked to the people at Alderson, and in order for me to be let out for Sue Lee's services, he would have to file a motion with my judge for a temporary furlough. "I'm working on it," he said, encouragement in his voice. Peter knew how important Sue Lee was to me—and to our entire family. He knew what kind of blow this was to our lives. He also understood that given my history with Judge Trauger, convincing her to accept the request might be difficult. Clearly, she was not my biggest fan, as evidenced by her decisions at the sentencing hearing. But he would try his hardest anyway; he always did. That's what I liked about Peter: he was never afraid of anybody saying "no."

The very next day after he submitted the motion, Judge Trauger sent it back, marked "DENIED." She said that because Sue Lee wasn't a member of my immediate family, there were not sufficient grounds to grant the furlough. I would have to watch her funeral on a DVD they would send—two entire weeks after it took place.

Of course, I had known how sick Sue Lee was; we all did. And I also knew that being stuck at Alderson, there were now hundreds of miles between us. But still, I never, *ever*, imagined that I wouldn't get the opportunity to say a proper goodbye to her, in the manner that most people do with a loved one.

When the DVD finally came, I remember going into one of the little private rooms in the chapel and watching the funeral in silence—Allie sitting beside me, there for support. I pressed the button on the old TV and saw everyone I cared about most appear on the screen. There was Pinky and my mother, my sister and brothers, my aunts and cousins. They were all there in Franklin, being led through the service with our pastor at Providence, Elder Mosley—moving together, through their tears, through their mourning. Celebrating, together, Sue Lee's life. And there I was, on the other side of the screen—and what felt like the other side of the world—grieving along with them but very much alone.

It was a layered kind of grief, stacked up with all the other losses that were impossible to process since walking through Alderson's gates: the loss of my old life and my future, the pain of being away from my family—especially during a time like this, when we all had to grapple with the reality that we would never see Sue Lee again.

But during this period of darkness, I also discovered that the women in the compound knew well what I was going through. Every woman there had walked into Alderson carrying the feeling of what she had lost with her. They all had experienced tragedy while they were here. Whether it was a death in the family or not being able to be there for a kid, there was always someone who'd been through something similar to what you were going through. And we all had to deal with that something—whatever it was—without our loved ones close by. So, in the absence of outside family, I learned that the women became each other's support. That in these hard moments, they were the ones you turned to because they were the only ones you had. Locked away from the outside world, they were the ones who you could talk to. They were the ones who could walk with you through whatever sorrow you had.

They were also the ones who knew—better than anyone else—that to survive, there were limits to how deeply you could feel. Because if you feel too much, you may succumb to the moment. And succumbing to the moment is something you simply cannot do. Because to survive, to stay strong, to do what you need to do to get your mind right, day by day, you must—must—keep moving.

And so, when the DVD of my great grandmother's funeral was over, I took it out of the player and returned it to Chaplain Walker, as I was told. I made the short walk back to my cubicle, accepting the hugs and words of encouragement from the women in my Range whom I'd grown to call friends.

And then I put my grief away and prepared for another day.

———

AFTER SIX MONTHS OF WORKING IN THE DINING ROOM AT CDR, I WAS itching to find another job—everyone at Alderson tried to switch out of the dining room as fast as they could.

During the weeks after my trial, when the reality of prison time became apparent, Peter and I did our research into various women's facilities. We looked through a book on federal prisons that Peter had in his office and specifically asked Judge Trauger to send me to Alderson because of the vocational and educational programs it advertised. There was another facility in my area that was much closer to home—a four-hour drive as opposed to an eight-hour one—but Alderson's programs seemed way more robust, and I was determined to stay as productive as I could with the time that I had.

But after my arrival, I quickly learned that the *actual* programs Alderson provided were a far cry from what was outlined in that federal prisons book. On the job front, most of us were pushed toward manual labor—working in masonry, or at the garage, or in landscaping—an area completely off-limits for me because of my allergies and sinuses. And as far as educational programs went, they were all about as "useful" as the typing class that was offered, which amounted to learning how to type on an old, dusty typewriter. In the year 2003.

Sorting through the lists, I finally landed on something that looked promising: maybe I could work as a library assistant. Alderson had both a leisure library and a law library. Being in either place, I thought, could definitely help me keep busy. And the law library came with the added advantage of giving me access to case law books, which might allow me to continue working on my own case. I had always loved books and reading. I submitted a request to my case manager to work at either place, but as quickly as I turned in my paperwork, I was turned away. Library positions were typically reserved for women with eighteen months or less left on their sentences, I was told. And plus, my case manager added, "We don't want you helping the other inmates with their legal matters."

Assisting inmates with their cases was forbidden at Alderson. And because of my particular background—my former job as a correctional officer, my criminal justice degree, my demonstrated interest in law school—I was told that putting me to work in the library just posed too much of a risk.

"What about cosmetology?" they would ask me, trying to redirect me elsewhere—anywhere—to more basic jobs. But I never liked doing my own hair, let alone someone else's.

———

EVENTUALLY, AFTER SOME BACK AND FORTH WITH MY CASE MANAGER, I was able to transfer out of CDR and land something in the Education building. It was a cleaning job—mopping and sweeping the floors of the admin offices and the GED and ESL classrooms, but at least I had some sort of proximity to knowledge. Every morning I reported to work at 8 a.m., with the six to eight other women I worked with. Usually, we were done with whatever tasks we had within a few hours, which meant that we were left with long stretches of time with not much to do.

CHAPTER 12

There was no leaving early if the day's work was done or going back to your cubicle to take a break. When you were at work, you stayed at work. And if we finished up early—which was often—we had to wait out the rest of the day in a designated room. Day after day, week after week, we cleaned the offices and the classrooms, then spent the entire rest of the shift—*hours* upon *hours*—watching the clock tick by. Some women slept, though sleeping wasn't allowed. Those of us awake would nudge the others when we heard the clacking of the officers' shoes coming toward the room we were in. Other women talked or read whatever books they brought in with them. But after a while, I needed to find something to *do* to keep myself from becoming completely stagnant.

Whenever I was cleaning the classrooms, I often crossed paths with Evelina—the teacher's aide for the GED classes, who was also serving out a sentence in the compound. In her time before Alderson, Evelina had been a nurse in the Washington, DC, area. As she set up for classes, we'd talk about our lives: her job, the careers we wanted to get back to—or in my case, the one I wanted to pursue. And then her students would start trickling in, and we'd both go back to our respective duties. I'd watch Evelina hand out workbooks, then get on with whatever lesson they were tackling that day.

After some time, I asked Evelina if maybe I could help her out, tutoring students, too. Before long, I was assisting women right beside her, helping with homework or test prep assignments— whatever extra help they might need outside of class. All new commits at Alderson without a high school diploma or equivalent were required to get their GED through the Adult Literacy Program—just as the non-English speakers were mandated to take ESL classes. While some of the women were just going through the motions in the classroom, others were genuinely eager to be there and to learn.

The GED requirement came down from the federal Bureau of Prisons—the BOP—which meant many (most) of the Education staff at Alderson were just going through the motions too. The teachers at Alderson offered the bare minimum and nothing more. Virtually none of them were invested in the women, in their lives or well-being. Any genuine care and effort always came from the other women at Alderson—from the teachers' aides, like Evelina, or volunteers like me, who actually wanted to see the people we were inside with succeed.

I remember one day, I was chatting with a group of women in the Education building, when Ms. Browning, the supervisor of the department, passed by. In every prison, there was always chatter about Congress passing some kind of early release initiative that might get us out sooner or of the possibility of reinstating federal parole, which was abolished in the early 1980s under the same restrictive crime control act that established mandatory minimums. In prison, acts of Congress were acts of faith, and many of us hung our hopes on the chance that some new law might be passed that would free us all. We were in the middle of a discussion along these lines when Ms. Browning stopped in front of us, overhearing the conversation we were having.

"Alderson would never do early release," she said, inserting herself in the middle of our talk. "You all are job security for us."

She offered up this statement like it was nothing—like it was a simple, readily known fact of life. In the prison system, your personhood is stripped down to dollars and cents. You become only as important as the job security you can provide for someone else; only as significant as the quota or the requirement those running the system needed to fulfill. And operating under this mentality, you are also so inconsequential that they felt that they could tell you these things to your face without batting an eye. To them, we barely existed.

In moments like these, I knew that we could only rely on ourselves—and each other—to survive.

chapter 13

WHEN I WASN'T FILLING UP MY TIME BY HELPING EVELINA IN THE Education building—or reading all the books I could get my hands on—I was working with Peter on my appeal. Since the trial had ended, he had committed himself to working on the next phases of my case free of charge. Because I was now in prison with very limited means, we were able to declare me "indigent," and Peter successfully petitioned to be appointed as my attorney. Six days after Judge Trauger sentenced me in the fall of 2002, we filed our motion for a direct appeal—meaning that we would be fighting both my felony conviction itself, as well as the judge's seven-year sentence. Armed with a plan, we began the necessary next steps in the process: requesting all seven volumes of transcripts from my trial, then sending them out to the Sixth Circuit—the court of appeals.

A few weeks after I arrived at Alderson, Peter and I began crafting the first major document in the process: a brief outlining all of the issues in the appeal. The basis of our case essentially came down to the fundamental fact that the government failed to provide sufficient evidence to support the aiding and abetting conviction or the deliberate ignorance argument—the *she-should-have known* defense. I did not know what I did not know; that truth would never change.

I spent hours holed up at the library, poring over case law books that might help bolster our arguments. If you were ever looking for me throughout the compound, nine times out of ten you could find me there, sitting at a table covered in books and briefs. After my shifts in the Education building ended, on nights and weekends—often right up until closing time—I was in that library, always digging deep into legal research.

It was there, working on the details of my own appeal, that I first learned how to Shepardize a case. In legal parlance, "Shepardizing" refers to the process of researching the outcomes of a given case—whether it was reaffirmed, overruled, questioned, or cited by different cases—by using a citation index called Shepard's Citations. The resource has been around since the 1870s, in book form, but as technology advanced, the process was eventually moved online—using research databases like Westlaw or LexisNexis. At Alderson, however, we didn't have computer access. I couldn't even access email for most of the time I was there. For us, if anybody wanted to do legal research, we had to do it old school, using often outdated copies of the Shepard's Citations books as a guide. But you work with what you have. And fortunately for me, if I couldn't find something I needed, I could always call Peter's assistants and ask them to send materials in.

Once I'd finished pulling together the research for my case, I'd send it back over to Peter to review, then we'd make plans to talk it all over. Several times throughout the process of creating and revising our briefs, he would get up early on Saturdays and make the eight-hour drive to Alderson to visit me in person. Sitting in the visitation area, we'd go over the brief he'd brought in with him, turning everything over piece by piece. Whenever Peter couldn't make the drive, we'd arrange to have lawyer phone calls, going back and forth over my research, further crafting and shaping the issues we were raising in the appeal. Peter even incorporated a few of my arguments into the briefs as they were finalized. These meetings with Peter, those late-night sessions in the library—they were all a sort of legal training grounds for me. I developed skills I would continue to draw from—again and again—in the years to come.

Over time, people in the compound got curious about what I was up to, seeing me spending day after day, night after night, working on my case. For many of the women at Alderson, their cases were over and done with by the time they had arrived. More often than not, after their arrests they pled guilty to whatever offense they were charged with, rather than go through the effort of a trial—likely facing even more time in prison after it was all over than the prosecution was offering up-front in exchange for a plea deal. And so, at the suggestion—and oftentimes the coercion—of their lawyers, they'd surrendered to the length of their sentences. Now, so many of the women I was imprisoned with were just waiting out their time, getting it over with so that they could one day, hopefully, continue on with their lives.

For this reason, talking about cases usually wasn't a big topic of conversation around the compound. It might come up during first meetings and introductions—I've been here for this long, or That's Ms. Mona, she's been locked up for thirty years—but for many, there just wasn't much left to say. I can count on one hand the number of women I actually talked to in full about my own situation or talked to about theirs. Some people knew the details of my case, others did not. There were a lot of women at Alderson whose case details I never knew, even though I got to know them well.

"Well, what are you here for?" someone might ask me, peering at the papers sprawled in front of me. "Aiding and abetting a conspiracy," I'd say. "Oh, So-and-So's here for conspiracy," came the typical response. There was rarely a detailed comparison of notes. But over time, you began to know the gist of why a person was there. And, piecing together bits of information shared in passing or mentioned along with a dozen other topics that might come up during the course of regular conversation, it was easy to identify a common thread. Pretty much everybody at Alderson, it seemed, was locked up for some damn conspiracy charge.

In 1988, as the War on Drugs was in full swing, Congress added conspiracy to commit a drug offense to the list of crimes eligible for mandatory minimum sentences, and when it did, the number of women facing drug convictions exploded. Because conspiracies cast such a wide net of involvement, any person thought to be a part of one could be held accountable for the entire group's activities—even if that person had zero knowledge of the actions or existence of other participants. And so—by the thousands—the girlfriends, wives, sisters, nieces, cousins, and mothers of high-level members of drug organizations were imprisoned just like their loved ones, often for little more than being in proximity to someone directly involved in the conspiracy. Even with marginal roles, the mandatory minimum sentencing laws guaranteed that they would face significant time behind bars: five, ten, twenty, thirty years—sometimes even life. Between 1980 and 2002, the year I was sentenced, the number of women placed in state and federal prisons skyrocketed—from 12,300 to over 96,000. And during that same year, 2002, women incarcerated for drug trafficking reached a record high.

Most of the women I met at Alderson were there for low-level, nonviolent drug-related crimes. Most were Black and brown, of course. The system is built to discriminate along racial lines. Many women were first-time offenders, like me. A lot of them were there under similar scenarios as mine—being close to a boyfriend or a husband or a family member whose actions took them down too. "This is fucked up," they'd often say whenever I disclosed my story. "You *really* don't belong here." The miscarriage of justice in my case, they agreed, felt incredibly wrong. Regardless of our various circumstances, everyone knew that the criminal justice system—and the unfair sentencing laws that governed it—had screwed us all. It had sought to destroy every single one of our lives in some kind of way.

But unlike me, because many of the women at Alderson had pled guilty, they had also by default given up their right to directly appeal their cases. The courts' judgment was irreversible for them. But in my case, women throughout the compound came to see a kind of hope. That maybe, just maybe, with my appeal, the system would do something right for a change.

After months of preparation, Peter finally submitted our appeal to the Sixth Circuit. Sunny Koshy and his prosecution team had the opportunity to respond, contesting the issues we made and bringing in their own case law examples to support their counterarguments. After that, we could submit a reply to their response, contesting their contestations—then they could do the same. Back and forth we went.

With every round of progress, the women at Alderson became increasingly invested in my case. Many of the other regulars at the library checked in about how things were going and where we were in the appeals process, as they continued to look into whatever research they could dig up for their own situations—in the cases where there was anything left to be done. Some people who checked in knew nothing about my case at all, other than that I had an appeal pending. But that was enough.

As I sat in the library, women would stroll in and out, asking for updates, sitting down to read whatever material was sprawled in front of me, debating arguments made by the prosecution during one of their replies. "This is bullshit," one woman might say, reading an argument Koshy was trying to make to uphold the deliberate ignorance defense. "That case clearly says the opposite," another person might add, thinking back to some other case she'd come across over the course of her own research. Afternoons in the library were often spent this way: a group of us, rifling through law books, discussing the details of case law. Putting more and more of ourselves into the hope that the right thing *had* to be done this time. That my conviction *had* to be overturned. Everybody wanted to believe that the criminal justice system was something other than what it was.

———

MONTHS PASSED, AND WE CONTINUED TO WAIT FOR WORD ABOUT NEXT steps for the appeal. Life at Alderson moved slowly. It drifted by—one hour into the next, one week after another—often turning the milestones that once meant something to you into just another day. Birthdays, anniversaries, holidays—we did our own little festivities, making cakes and other things we could throw together with items bought from the commissary. But for me and for many of the women at Alderson, I think these events were also painful reminders: *Another year older and I never thought my life would end up this way; it's my child's graduation; or it's my grandparents' anniversary; or it's my father's retirement—and I can't celebrate with them because they're out there, and I'm in here.* So, you do what you have to do to get through it; compartmentalizing your feelings, however you can, to get through each day—especially the ones that hold a little extra significance.

Because of the hours-long drive from Franklin to Alderson, in-person visits with my family were rare. My mom and Pinky did make the trip a few times, including once at Easter during the one and only time families were allowed inside on the grounds for a special Sunday service at the chapel. I didn't see my father at all, or my friends, or any of my siblings. But my family sent cards and wrote letters, and I talked to them all as much as I could over the phone, with the limited number of allotted minutes we had. Two hundred and forty minutes per month, an extra hundred during the holidays. Because the lines to use the phones were often long, you might only get fifteen good minutes of quality time in before you were kicked off for the next person. Plus, calls were extremely expensive, so these catchups, when they happened, were often short by necessity—the minutes racking up money that your family had to help out to pay.

But we all got by, as best we could. I remember one call with Anitra; we were talking about prison, and how there were more than just physical prisons you could be in. There were emotional prisons, spiritual prisons, mental prisons—sometimes of your own making. I saw how easily that could happen, especially in a place like this. I knew that to avoid getting stuck, to avoid feeling trapped, I had to keep pushing myself.

With the heavy-lifting work of constructing the briefs behind us, I was left—again—with long stretches of time with nothing to do. During the course of requesting materials and scheduling lawyer meetings with Peter, I often coordinated with his legal assistants, and in the process we became close. Sete had plans to attend law school too, and we talked about it often during our calls. But when she decided to switch lanes and get a business degree instead, she sent me her LSAT books since she no longer had much use for them. After work, in the evenings and on weekends, I prepped for the LSAT with the books Sete sent me. I was happy to put this constructive time in. Whenever I finally left Alderson, I knew I could hit the ground running on my path to becoming a lawyer.

Sete eventually left Peter's office, and soon another young woman named Amber took over her job. She was smart, sharp, and ambitious, and we quickly hit it off. Whenever I called to get updates on the case, we would fall into conversations about our aspirations.

We talked about motivating each other through the LSAT and even joked about going to law school together one day, and becoming roommates.

Legal practice, the law, becoming an attorney—these things were always at the forefront of my mind. Especially during those months I'd spent with Peter, digging into the legal system to craft the arguments and issues that would help shape my own appeal. There was so much to learn, so much I wanted to do.

Between studying for the LSAT and still tutoring with Evelina from time to time, I began to take on a new activity: helping a few women at Alderson with their cases. I did this quietly with one of my friends and a few women who lived in my unit. I didn't really want to put it out there because there were other women who had already established themselves as doing this kind of work around the compound.

In every jail and prison, you have your prison lawyers. People in these facilities who do legal research or write habeas corpus letters—petitions submitted to the court to determine if the person's imprisonment is unlawful—for other folks inside. Sylvia was one of the go-to women who did this at Alderson. She was actually a former lawyer from Virginia, who was serving a seven- to nine-year sentence. Sylvia and I had gotten close since I first arrived on the compound; she was also one of the people I chatted to the most about the larger goings-on in Congress: what it might be saying or doing legislation-wise that could potentially free us all from our sentences. And there was always something Congress *may be* doing—a new early release bill that was maybe coming down the pike or a new initiative aimed at abolishing mandatory minimums. Many of the women became obsessed with these bits of news—of hope—and talked about them constantly.

CHAPTER 13

"Hey, Keeda—what's the word?" Sylvia would call out to me every single time she saw me around the compound. Then we'd stand around for the next thirty minutes shooting the shit, exchanging theories about what we thought might be done.

Because I had a direct line to my attorney, people came to know me as someone who had, or could get, information. Whenever I'd call Peter's office and ask Amber for articles about proposed bills advocating for the reinstatement of federal parole or giving certain people early release, she'd send me multiple copies so I could pass them around.

But, of course, no one ever got out early. No bills that reconsidered the issue of federal parole got very far. Congress wasn't doing anything but locking people up. Ms. Browning—the woman overseeing Alderson's Education Department, the one who forced herself into our conversation that day while we were talking about early release bills—she was right. There was just too much riding on us staying exactly where we were.

Gradually, other women around the compound started reaching out and asking for advice. People knew or found out that I had a degree in criminal justice and psychology—on top of always seeing me in the library, or in the visiting building with Peter, working on my appeal. Bit by bit, I began learning more about some of the other women's situations. Hearing their stories, listening to their issues. Learning about what their lawyers didn't—or wouldn't—do that could have given them a better shot or a fairer chance. Then, I took to my research, trying to help them out as best as I could. And if Alderson's law library didn't have some piece of research they needed—which was often—I would call up Peter's office and talk to Amber, asking her to send me things, as she'd done so many times for my own case.

In this way, I established a kind of rhythm: breaking up the monotony, the waiting, by pouring myself into the future—my future studies in law school and the futures of a few other women with me on the inside whom I tried to help.

And then one day, after what seemed like endless silence, we got the word we'd been waiting for. Peter was to argue my appeal in front of the Sixth Circuit. *One step closer*, I thought.

The day his argument was scheduled, I stayed occupied, going through the motions: moving through my tasks at work, reporting for Count Times and meals, spending time in the chapel or with the library crew in the Rec building. Trading hopeful chatter with the other women in the compound who had come to hold my case close as if it were their own.

I talked to Peter the next day, and he went over everything that happened. Oral arguments were quick—fifteen minutes max—enough time to go through the top-line issues in your appeal and leave a few minutes at the end for rebuttals from the prosecution or follow-up questions. He felt good about how it all went. But there would still be a waiting period before the court came to its final decision.

More time went by in silence.

chapter 14

N 2004, WHILE MY CASE MADE ITS WAY THROUGH THE APPEALS PRO-
cess, the entire US legal system was suddenly turned upside down.
Courts dissolved into complete chaos. Judges from state to state were
in disagreement about how to move forward. The lines around certain processes and procedures as we knew them became blurred.

The issue came down to the constitutionality of the country's
federal sentencing guidelines—a system that had been seen as the
undisputed law of the land for the past twenty years.

Originally enacted in 1984, the guidelines were made in response
to what had been observed as disparities in the federal court system.
Judges were noticing that people with the same criminal history,
charged with the same crime, were being sentenced very differently
depending on what district they were in and which judge was presiding over their cases. The guidelines, they initially thought, would
be a way to codify and "equalize" judges' decision-making by making them all adhere to the same rubric to determine sentencing. The
solution would mandate that every judge use the same set of measures
to decide a person's fate. This was why during the sentencing hearing

in my case, while the jury convicted me of the mandatory minimum sentence of sixty months, after adding in factors about my role in the conspiracy as argued by the prosecution—Judge Trauger determined that my conviction warranted a sentence between seventy-eight to ninety-seven months, per calculations set by the federal sentencing guidelines.

In their initial conception, these guidelines were meant to be mandatory—meaning that judges were required to impose a sentence within the range that had been explicitly determined by the guidelines. But they also allowed judges to increase a person's sentence beyond the guidelines' maximum determination based on facts not considered by the jury or admitted to by the defendant.

And then, in 2004, new litigation through two high-profile federal court cases—*Blakely v. Washington*, followed by *Booker v. Fanfan*—challenged the guidelines' basis, exposing their possible unconstitutionality. Both raised the fundamental question of whether they violated a person's Sixth Amendment right to a fair trial. If these guidelines allowed judges to enhance a person's sentence based on facts not proven beyond a reasonable doubt to a jury, how could they really be fair? In this scenario, a judge could increase a person's sentence using facts taken into consideration by the judge alone.

The Blakely case, decided in June 2004, confirmed that the guidelines were indeed in violation of the Sixth Amendment. Then, the *Booker v. Fanfan* case, argued four months later, forced the Supreme Court judges to figure out how to revise the guidelines to accord with the Constitution. They later decided that to address the guidelines' Sixth Amendment violation, all language that made them mandatory would be invalidated. Going forward—according to a monumental decision—the federal sentencing guidelines would now be advisory. Judges could use them to aid in their decision-making, but they would no longer be bound to enforce the sentences the guidelines dictated.

Suddenly, thousands upon thousands of federal cases were being reconsidered in light of this historic ruling—including my own.

"Okay, this is confusing." I was on the phone with Peter's assistant Amber one day, getting an update on what was going on with the case since Peter had delivered oral arguments.

"It looks like they granted the appeal, and then they went back and denied it." In the midst of everything going on, the lower courts now didn't quite know what to do with my case. With the latest news coming out of Washington, there was clear cause to reconsider my sentence—but how exactly, no one in the lower courts knew.

After this, the confusion resulted in eight more long months of my case being in limbo. The appeal volleyed around the Court of Appeals for the Sixth Circuit, until we eventually—finally—got word that the ultimate decision would be placed before the highest court in the land: the Supreme Court.

On January 25, 2005, Peter received a letter of response from the Supreme Court itself about our motion to appeal. "The judgment is vacated," they wrote. "And the case is remanded to the United States Court of Appeals for the Sixth Circuit for further consideration in light of *Booker*." I still have a copy of that letter to this day.

We had won. Our appeal was granted.

My case was sent back to the Sixth Circuit, as ordered—which then determined that it would be sent *back* to the District Court for the Middle District of Tennessee.

There, I would sit face-to-face with Judge Aleta Trauger again for a resentencing hearing.

———

THANK YOU, GOD, I THOUGHT TO MYSELF WHEN I GOT THE NEWS. I HAD prayed for this moment—I had put my entire faith into this moment. Since the day this nightmare began, I had been carried through by the belief that somehow, some way, God would make sure everything worked out in my favor. That, in the end, my course would be righted, the slate wiped clean as it should have been all along. And now, with this resentencing hearing—with the Supreme Court itself on my side—my moment had finally come. The judge would have no choice but to do the right thing.

I was going home. I was convinced of it.

The women at Alderson were convinced, too. They were deeply encouraged—this glimmer of hope we all wanted to believe in was now coming true. So many of the others' cases may have been over—their right to appeal extinguished the moment too many of them were pressured into pleading guilty. They had been wronged by the system just as I had been. But my liberty—my exoneration—would be their victory too.

In the weeks leading up to the hearing, I started giving away most of the stuff I'd gathered over the last two years I'd been there and began saying my goodbyes. Amber, also sure that we would soon be closing the book on my case for good, began making my postrelease plans with me. She would soon be leaving, and the timing would be perfect for me to take over her position as Peter's legal secretary while I prepared for law school. Peter and I had become quite a team throughout this long process, fighting so many battles with my case—working through arguments and briefs, analyzing case law. He recognized my potential; he believed in me. And he knew that, regardless of the potential barriers ahead, I would be undaunted in my pursuit of a career in the law. So, together, we made plans for my future.

To prepare for the resentencing, he asked that we collect testimonies from the people I was closest with to give Judge Trauger a sense of my character and conduct since she had seen me last. We submitted letters from my family—my parents and Pinky, my younger brother Johnathon and my aunt Shawn; from close friends like Christana; from members of my church; and, of course, from women at Alderson.

On top of these, we forwarded work reports from my time in CDR and the Education building, which evaluated my job performance. In every single one, I was given above-average marks.

With this character package complete, and all my belongings given away or packed up in R&D, I set out on the long journey back home. Back to Tennessee. Back to receive my overdue fair judgment—the hopes and wishes and prayers of so many of the women at Alderson guiding me forward.

———

AFTER BEING INSIDE ALDERSON FOR A LITTLE OVER TWO YEARS, MY resentencing hearing was finally scheduled for May 19, 2005, in Nashville. But I left Alderson weeks ahead of time to get there. The transportation process in the federal prison system is a long, daunting trek that often involves many intermittent stops before reaching the final destination. It was a kind of trial before the trial, I would soon discover. One more test in a long series, designed to break you down.

On the morning I left the compound, I got into a transport van with a few other women bound for impending court dates and drove about an hour away to the nearest airport in Beckley, West Virginia. From there, we were herded onto a Boeing 737 by armed US Marshals, shackled and handcuffed, then shackled again to the floor after we were escorted to our seats.

It was my very first time on a plane. I couldn't believe that my introduction to flying would not be onboard some commercial flight, but through the Justice Prisoner and Alien Transportation System airline—or JPATS, also commonly referred to as "Con Air."

There were marshals carrying rifles stationed throughout the cabin and only a few other women onboard. We were seated toward the front of the aircraft, while the men—the vast majority of them Black—filled up the rest of the plane, taking their places in the middle and back rows. I remember being struck by that image: seeing a plane full of shackled Black men—one after another, after another— bound for prisons across the country. Shackled in the same way we were on the auction block centuries before, bound for prisons called by another name.

It's a legacy of oppression that has followed us throughout each decade, morphing and shifting in different ways. Today, Black men are six times as likely to be incarcerated as white men. In 2005, the year I witnessed so many of them filling up that plane, about 8.1 percent of the total Black male population between the ages of twenty-five and twenty-nine were in state or federal prison, as opposed to just 1.1 percent of white males.

Here, on this plane filled with incarcerated people who looked like me and my family and friends, I witnessed those statistics come startlingly to life.

As the airplane rumbled down the runway, I felt my body tighten— my fear of flying taking over my thoughts. My ears popped during the takeoff, and I fought back nausea and nervousness throughout the entire ride. After several hours in the air, we started a bumpy, dizzying descent into Oklahoma City, Oklahoma.

Every person being transported throughout the federal prison system has to make a stop at a facility in Oklahoma City at some point during their journey. It is the system's transit hub; the place where everyone is processed before being spit out again onto buses or planes to get to wherever the ultimate destination is. I was in

Oklahoma for about a week, sleeping in a cell, before boarding another plane that would take me to yet another detention center. This time in Mason, Tennessee—a small town about two and a half hours outside of Nashville.

The West Tennessee Detention Facility was a private prison, owned and operated by the Corrections Corporation of America (CCA) (now called CoreCivic). CCA was known for launching the era of corporate-run prisons in the early 1980s—in direct response to government-run facilities being pushed to overcrowding as the War on Drugs got underway. As a result, CCA prisons *directly* influenced the rise of incarceration as a multibillion-dollar business. With profits driven by high occupancy rates, the private prison industry is also a major contributing factor to the 500 percent increase in incarceration the United States has experienced over the last four decades. CCA detention centers developed a notorious reputation for their horrible conditions—filthy living quarters, mistreatment and abuse, overall lack of safety and health care for those imprisoned. And the West Tennessee Detention Facility in Mason was no exception.

Being processed inside on my first day, I was given a dingy towel, a thin cotton blanket, and used prison-issued underwear that I refused to wear. *Used.* Underwear. Many of the women at the Mason facility chose against this option, considering it more hygienic to either wash the pair you came in with or wear no undergarments at all, rather than put on the filthy ones handed over to us when we got inside.

The facility was dirty, sticky, and grimy, with insects—of all kinds—crawling everywhere. For weeks I sat in a small cell in Mason, biding my time—reading mostly—waiting for someone to come in and say it was time for me to leave, so I could continue on to the next stop.

One afternoon a few days in, I was lying on my top bunk, deep in the pages of a book, when I heard someone call my name from the entrance of the cell. "Keeda Haynes." It was spoken more like a statement than a question. I looked up from my reading to see who it was. "I thought that was you," the woman said, leaning against the concrete opening to the cell.

"Amy?" I replied.

Since this entire roller coaster began, I could now count two chance encounters with people from my hometown while I was trapped in the criminal justice system: Heather Goodman from my high school was the first, back in the Williamson County Jail in Franklin during that initial weekend of my arrest; and now, here in Mason, Amy was the second. Amy was a year younger than I was—more a friend of my little brother's—but I'd known her since junior high.

She told me that she had walked by my door a couple of times over the last few days, but she couldn't figure out whether it was really me. Every time she passed she'd linger at my door, seeing me on the top bunk. *That looks like Keeda*, she'd say to herself, trying to get a closer look. *But no. Keeda would never be in prison.* Another day would pass, and she'd look in on me again, thinking, *It can't be her . . . But wow, she looks just like Keeda Haynes.* Finally, that day, she announced herself at my door, seeking to put an end to her suspicions once and for all.

Amy had been in Mason for several weeks, moving through the prison transport process just like I was. She was locked up, she said, because she had tried to rob a bank while high on drugs. They hadn't given her as much time as they could have, and they also offered her the option of going through a drug program to get some help before going home.

"Oh, Judge Trauger! That's the same judge I had," she said when I began talking about my situation. "She's so great—and so nice!" Clearly, our experiences with this same judge couldn't have been more different. Amy had tried to rob a bank—and freely admitted to it—and had been given far less time to serve than I had. "Judge Trauger's going to do the right thing, Keeda," she reassured me. "She'll let you go home—she's got to." Amy was the type of person who always wanted to believe the best in everybody. "I know she will."

I hoped Amy was right. But even if Judge Trauger didn't want to do the right thing, I knew the law was on my side. At least I hoped it was.

A few days later, I learned that I was finally going to be taken to the next stop on my journey. I left Mason to travel to yet another jail—this time in Nashville. Another step closer. I was beyond ready to leave this dingy, dark place—and its used underwear—behind.

chapter 15

A FEW DAYS LATER, PULLING UP TO THE CORRECTIONAL DEVELOP-ment Center (CDC) building—where most pretrial prisoners in Nashville were placed—I took in the familiar surroundings. The CDC building had changed since I last worked inside it as a correctional officer. A lot had changed in those four years. I had spent most of my time as a CO in this building; I'd driven countless times up and down Harding Place, the road leading into the facility. But I'd never done it in handcuffs or with shackles on my feet. I'd never done it as inmate 00017-011.

I arrived in front of their newly created women's facility, CDC-F—nonexistent during my time there—and waited to be escorted inside. A few minutes later a CO emerged to take me in. When I saw his face, I immediately registered him as someone I knew. It was Bogle, a lieutenant while I was working in the jail, though not one I reported to directly. As we walked side by side up the pathway toward the door, we didn't pass a single word between us. But I knew he recognized me too. Every so often, I caught him glancing at me out of the corner of his eye, searching my face to place me.

"I thought it was you," he said later, standing in the entryway of my cell—now sure that it was actually me. That was it. He then turned back around and left the same way he came.

It was here, in a place that layered so much of the life I once had, on top of a very different one that was forced upon me, that I spent my final days before the resentencing hearing was scheduled to take place.

———

ON THE AFTERNOON OF MAY 19, 2005, I FILED INTO THE COURTROOM wearing a blue prison-issued jumpsuit, "DCSO" (Davidson County Sheriff's Office) stamped in big letters on the back. I was sure of the fate that was awaiting me. On the other side of this hearing, I knew I would be walking out as a free woman. I was ready. Ready to get this over with. Ready to go home.

I glanced around the room, seeing Peter and Sunny Koshy and Judge Trauger—all prepared to go to bat from their respective sides. I turned a little more and also spotted my mother and Pinky sitting calmly behind me. They were joined by my cousin Jamese, who had also come to support me for this important moment. Looking into their faces, I was reminded of everything I missed; of why it was so important to sometimes push away the images of the people you love while you're locked away from them. It hurt too much to see them. But soon—very soon—this nightmare would all be over, and I would be with the people I loved once again.

Sitting high above the rest of us from her perch in the courtroom, Judge Trauger opened a folder in front of her and began by walking us through the life of my case since I'd last seen her two and a half years before: her initial ruling; the twists and turns of my appeal; and the Supreme Court's ultimate decision to vacate her original judgment in light of the *Booker v. Fanfan* decision, declaring the federal sentencing guidelines no longer mandatory under new reforms.

This was Judge Trauger's opportunity—and ours—to start over. To finally make this terrible wrong right.

"The court is not inclined to sentence Ms. Haynes below the mandatory minimum of 60 months," Judge Trauger announced at the end of her opening summary—before either side had a chance to speak. "So if for other purposes you want to go forward . . . I will hear the proof," she continued, looking at Peter. "But I'm just telling you at the front end, I'm not inclined to go below the 60 months."

I felt my stomach drop. Endless hours of hard work and research—*years* of legal battles lost and won to get to this appeal—and Judge Trauger was saying to us within the opening *minutes* of the hearing that she would not be keeping an open mind when it came to our arguments. That in reconsidering her judgment, as the Supreme Court and the Court of Appeals for the Sixth Circuit had ordered her to do, entertaining anything less than my original mandatory minimum sentence was simply out of the question.

At that moment I knew that this day—like so many others before—would be another hard fight for my life.

Sensing where the wind was now blowing, Peter—forever the fighter—dug in. He was prepared to say what he came to say, regardless of Judge Trauger's intentions. "Yes, Your Honor," he answered, keeping his voice calm and his gaze level. "I just want to flesh out the argument I put in my position paper. With the court's permission," he said, organizing his papers, "I had some things that I wanted to discuss with the court."

Ahead of the hearing, Peter submitted a position paper that outlined two pathways Judge Trauger could consider to lessen my sentence. The first went back to the verdict form the jury was given when they were tasked with coming up with their decision. Because that form didn't allow jurors to specify the amount of marijuana attributable solely to me, the number they were left to consider—"one hundred kilograms or more"—automatically triggered my mandatory minimum sentence of five years.

The issue for jurors to consider was not *How much was Keeda Haynes responsible for?* or *Was Keeda Haynes responsible for one hundred kilograms or more of marijuana?* The question they were given was whether I had participated in a conspiracy involving one hundred kilograms or more of marijuana. There was no disputing, from either side, that the extent of C and his cousins' operation involved more than one hundred kilograms of marijuana. It was a simple, obvious fact of the case. But because of the design of the verdict form, it was a question they had no choice but to answer in the affirmative once they'd found me guilty of aiding and abetting. The jurors had six questions to rule on about my involvement, and they answered negatively on every one of them—but that one. By reconsidering this crucial factor, we hoped that Judge Trauger might arrive at a different judgment.

The second pathway to a lesser sentence involved what's called the safety valve provision, which allows judges to sentence people below the mandatory minimum they've been convicted of, provided they meet some key criteria: they must have a minimal past criminal record; played only a minor role in the offense; did not use violence of any kind in the offense; and—most important in my case—they must have told the government all they knew of the offense and any related misconduct.

Arguing for the use of the safety valve in my case, Peter reiterated that I passed all the requirements with flying colors—including the last prong that involved telling the government the whole truth. My voluntary testimony to agent Dan Kennedy during that FBI interview from March 2001 proved it. During Peter's cross-examination of Kennedy during the trial, "He indicated that the information . . .

[I] provided him was consistent with the objective facts of the case."
And, he reminded the court, during the entire course of the trial
proceedings, not a *single* one of the witnesses who testified could
look the jury in the eye and say, 'I told her there was marijuana in the
package,' or 'she told me there was marijuana in the package.'"

I had told the only truth I knew. And because I insisted on that
truth—reiterating, again and again, that I was reassured into believing C's stories—I was ultimately judged a liar. Judged a liar then,
during my trial three years ago, and apparently again now in this
courtroom, as I fought for my freedom once more.

"The court does not believe that Ms. Haynes did not know that
there was illegality going on," Judge Trauger said after listening to
Peter's and Sunny Koshy's rebuttals.

"I simply just don't believe her."

No matter the evidence presented, she remained unconvinced by
Peter's arguments. Her mind remained firmly made up.

"And so at this point, I'm prepared to hear any statement that Ms.
Haynes wishes to make," Judge Trauger said with finality, turning to
me. "Any testimony she wants to put on in terms of convincing me
that I should not reaffirm my original sentence."

I felt like we were back in the same nightmare of the sentencing
hearing: me, again, begging for whatever scraps of mercy this judge
might have left for me. But unlike last time, I had prepared my speech
in advance. I wrote it before I had entered the courtroom—before
Judge Trauger's judgment. Even with the writing on the wall, I was
prepared to push forward, just as Peter had.

Although I turned to address the judge, as I looked over to where
my mother, grandmother, and cousin sat, I spoke to them instead:

"In spite of the negative things this situation has produced, my
family has still stood by me. Their love and their support has always
been there. When there were times that I felt like I couldn't make it

another day, they encouraged me, and their support was there. There was never a time that I doubted their support and everything they did for me. They were faithful. They made sacrifice upon sacrifice for me, and I can never repay them for that. All I could do is just extend my sincerest gratitude.

"This situation was designed to tear my family apart. But in actuality, the exact opposite is what has happened. We have gotten closer together in the past three years. Even with the death of my great-grandmother, who I never got to say goodbye to or apologize to for having involved her in this situation, we still have grown closer and closer.

"It is only by the grace of God that we have been able to get through this as a family. And I thank Him every day for my family and for their love and support."

I then turned to Peter, who had worked and fought so hard to get us here. Who had shown up for me, day after day, without fail. "He has blessed me beyond anything he could possibly imagine. Peter, I just want to thank you for that."

Every person facing this unforgiving system should have a lawyer like Peter, I thought. Everyone should have someone to show up for them in this way, whether they can afford the representation or not.

I thought about how much I could have lost, the kind of person I could have turned into, during the course of the trials over the last few years.

"I thank God that in the midst of all of this, I haven't become bitter and angry or distrustful, but instead I have become mature, wiser, and more cautious in my relationships with people. . . . When this whole situation began, I was only 19 years old. I didn't really know anything about life or relationships. . . . If I could go back, I definitely would. . . . But I can't. Now all I can do is take all the things that I have learned, and the changes I have made, and move forward and be a better person. Given the opportunity to be released, the plans that I have for my future is to continue my studies for the LSAT and attend law school and be the best attorney that I can be."

I flipped to the last page of my letter and took a breath.

"If I can prevent one person from having to walk down this road that I have been down by sharing my experience and what I have learned, then it would all be worth it."

I knew that when I said this last part, Judge Trauger would likely interpret it to mean that I wanted to prevent others from making the same mistake that I had, to be more "aware" of the kind of trouble I was potentially getting myself into. But, of course, that's not at all what I meant.

By "walking down this road," by "sharing my experience and what I have learned," I didn't mean unknowingly getting caught up in C and his cousins' drug conspiracy. When I said those words during my resentencing hearing, I was declaring that I would do everything in my power to prevent someone else from being taken advantage of by the system in the way that it took advantage of me. What would make this hell worth it for me was sharing the hard lessons I should never have had to learn. And turning those lessons into action.

After reading the letters from my loved ones, seeing my work reports, hearing my own testimony, the judge thought that I had made good use of my time. She said she even believed that I had probably gotten all that I was going to get out of my imprisonment. But she also remained firm in the judgment she'd made about me years ago—convinced, still, that I had lied to myself, and therefore to the government. And for that, in her eyes, my punishment had yet to be fully paid.

In the end, none of the work we did was quite enough. Judge Trauger reduced the original sentence she handed to me over two years ago from seven years to five—the mandatory minimum for my conviction.

I now had eighteen more months left to serve.

Just as she'd done at my initial sentencing, Judge Trauger ultimately wanted me to conform to her story. She wanted me to have one like Amy's—someone who'd lost her way to bad behavior and made some big mistakes but was now ready to repent and do better. Stories like Amy's "deserved" leniency because stories like Amy's made sense to Judge Trauger. But stories like mine did not—or, at least, not enough to justify setting me free.

"I feel you have turned around, Ms. Haynes," she said, looking at me over her glasses. "And I've given you the break that I feel like I can give you." The "break" of a permanent felony conviction on my record. The "mercy" of eighteen months left to serve in a place that had already taken away years of my life.

"I feel that we will not see you again in the criminal justice system, will we?"

"No, ma'am," I responded. *No, you damn sure would not.* At least not in the manner she might have been thinking. My journey to take on the justice system was only beginning.

chapter 16

THE ROAD BACK TO ALDERSON WAS TWICE AS LONG AS THE ONE I
took to leave for the resentencing. Without the urgency of deliv-
ering me to a scheduled court date, the federal transport system took
its time. I went back to CDC in Nashville for a while; then back to
Mason, where Amy continued to wait. About a month passed before
Amy and I both left, traveling back to the transit hub in Oklahoma
City. And then, after several weeks there, we finally parted ways. Amy
went to a facility in Kentucky, while I set out on my last leg back to
West Virginia.

When I finally stepped foot again on the compound, at least two
months had gone by since I'd left for the resentencing hearing. I
looked around in disbelief at my surroundings: the familiar hills and
sidewalks, the buildings and the trees, the Blue Ridge Mountains
in the distance. I wasn't supposed to be here for another eighteen
months. Another year and a half. I was only supposed to have come
back to Alderson long enough to retrieve my remaining things and
leave for good. By this point, I was supposed to be well on my way
toward putting all of this behind me, picking my life back up from

where it was taken away. I was supposed to be entering the phase where I was recalling this period of time as nothing more than a horrible nightmare that I had thankfully woken up from.

But instead, here I was. Still living inside this bad dream that I couldn't seem to shake.

My friends on the compound were eager to hear the news of what had happened. There was no way that the outcome of the appeal could have traveled back to them before I got there, so for these two months, they were waiting too. Hoping that the courts had gotten it right. Believing that they would. When I told them about Judge Trauger's decision—that she reduced my mandatory minimum sentence to five years—although it wasn't the outcome we had all hoped for, they were genuinely happy for me. Anything that allows you to get out of prison early is a win.

Yes, my sentence had been reduced from seven years to five. It was *something*—and not at all unsignificant. A lot of the women at Alderson never even got the kind of opportunity I did to appeal. So many of their cases were closed for good. But I thought the system was supposed to have made this clear-cut wrong, right. The mistake of my conviction was supposed to be fixed. Instead—even with the Supreme Court on my side—I was back here at Alderson. My outcome proved to me that the system had not only failed me, but that the reality of it, every single aspect of it, was a failure.

The hard truth of the matter was that the criminal justice system would continue to fail us all because that's what it was designed to do. My return to the compound meant coming to grips with this brutal fact. A fact that a lot of the women on the compound already knew.

All of us who entered the criminal justice system in the 1990s and early 2000s, we knew *The New Jim Crow* before Michelle Alexander wrote about it. We knew it because we experienced it. That Black and brown people were coming into prison with way longer sentences than white people. That people of color were often prevented from accessing the same resources freely given to whites, like drug programs, that would get time knocked off their sentences. The dominant narrative had already been decided: Black people committed crimes just because they were Black. White people committed crimes because they needed help.

It was clear that the system was rigged. Had been rigged all along. The outcome of my resentencing proved, once and for all, that if your skin was brown, like mine was—no matter what—you would lose.

In the days and weeks after I returned to the compound, I descended into a dark place. I tried to have some perspective: That Peter and I wouldn't stop fighting; we would be appealing the case again. The felony conviction was now a moot point; it looked like it would be attached to me for the rest of my life. But we could at least try to challenge Judge Trauger's sentence once again, since she could have given me below the mandatory minimum but ultimately decided against it.

But it was the reality of the felony label that I kept getting stuck on. It didn't make sense. Since the day I had been thrown into the criminal justice system, I spent every day knowing that this was not a label I would have to live with forever. That somehow God would allow for some outcome that would make it go away. I trusted it; I believed it. But now a different reality was presenting itself, and there was no way around it. It kept getting in the way, interrupting everything I thought I knew.

I am nothing if not rooted and grounded in my faith. And I knew God would not allow me to move through the rest of my days carrying this conviction. But here I was, struggling to come to terms with what having a felony would mean for me. Trying to imagine what future hardships lay ahead—how the stigma of this label would touch each and every part of my life. How it might create more hurdles for me to cross over; how it might impact my relationships, my schooling, my career. Suddenly, these thoughts came into overwhelming focus. How could I face a future I never thought I would have to contemplate? How do I move forward in my faith when what I have been trusting and believing in did not come to pass?

The plans that were perfectly lined up for me to take over Amber's position as Peter's assistant? Gone. My time line to take the LSAT and continue onto law school? Disrupted. My goal to practice law afterward? Unclear. Even a few women at Alderson questioned whether I would be able to pursue a career in law with a felony conviction on my record. My whole life—every grounding force that kept me moving—hung in the balance of this new uncertainty.

I floated through my days, one unsure step after the next.

During this time, I still tried to find solace in the chapel. Most Sundays since arriving at Alderson a different ministry group from outside the prison would come in to do the service. As part of the program, the Alderson Praise and Worship Team would lead us in song.

Our choir, Echoes of Harmony, led by Peaches, would sing. Usually one of our dance teams, led by China and Yolanda, would also perform.

On the Sundays when the visiting ministry was from a Black church, *everybody* at Alderson came to the chapel. Those events got so big that sometimes they had to hold them in the gym instead to accommodate the crowds.

During one such Sunday, my friends and I headed to the chapel after brunch as usual, this time to see a visiting ministry from DC that everyone at Alderson loved. The place was packed, and we made our way to the front of the chapel to a row of folding chairs that had been set up to address the overflow. At one point during the service,

Ages of Praise, the elderly women's dance team at Alderson, took to the stage and began to perform a Donnie McClurkin song.

I know that faith is easy when everything is going well, the song began.

But can you still believe in Me when your life's a living hell?

Something began to take hold of me with each verse; the words felt close, intimate—like they were not just lyrics to a song but words addressed specifically to me.

In that moment, I felt certain that God was speaking to me. In the face of so much that had seemingly unraveled around me, so much that was out of my control, He was simply asking: *Will you trust Me?*

Up until my resentencing hearing—really and truly—my faith had not been tested. *Okay, Lord,* I thought, after the initial conviction, after the setbacks along the way. *Well, I may have lost this round, but I'm going to win this appeal. It's going to be okay.*

I was not going to have that thorn in my flesh that Paul talks about in the Bible.

But when the judgment did not go my way, when God did not go through with what I thought we'd both agreed on, it was as if He'd left that thorn there—like He did with Paul. *Will you trust me?* the song went.

The question, I realized, was an invitation to surrender. God left the thorn in Paul's flesh to buffet him and to humble him. And to act as a reminder to Paul that he was going to have to depend on Him.

I had grown up in church all my life. I had studied the Bible and took wisdom from the scripture. But I never had to define my faith on my own. I never had to break it apart and put it back together again in a way that pushed me to expand my understanding of what's possible. That forced me to put my trust in a future I could not see.

But standing at this crossroads, I had to make a choice: Do I continue to wrestle with the unknown? Or do I choose to surrender and trust Him with my life? Sitting there in the chapel, inside the place where I had been imprisoned for the last nearly three years, I closed my eyes. *All I can see is this moment*, I said to myself. *And in this moment I have a conviction on my record.*

But God sees further than that.

I had never lost my faith, but in that moment I knew I had to redefine it.

The thought felt like a reckoning. The point, I finally understood, wasn't that everything would be okay if things went one specific way. It was that I could *choose* to have faith, hope, belief, regardless of whether I could put my hands around the outcome and feel it for myself. The label, the barriers, the resentence—there was a bigger plan for all of it. All I had to do was keep going, following His trust. My job was not to know the future, it was to move in God's vision for it, even if I couldn't fully see what it was.

Almost immediately, as this new truth worked its way through me, I felt at peace. A peace that truly surpassed all understanding. I was seized by a different courage, a deeper channel of motivation. From that moment on, I knew I wasn't just depending on myself to make things happen. I knew that the journey ahead may be unknown, but it wasn't only up to me to see my way through it. Things were as they were for a reason. I would use it all as fuel—as momentum.

Nothing, and no one, could deter me now.

chapter 17

I APPROACHED MY LAST STRETCH OF TIME AT ALDERSON WITH A NEW kind of focus. I continued to study for the LSAT. Peter and I also started a conversation about working as his assistant. He assured me that I would have a job at his office when I got out—he would make absolutely sure of it. After rounds and rounds of denials, I was also finally approved to join Alderson's Library Assistant Program. I transitioned out of the Education building and began working both in the compound's law and leisure libraries, officially.

Throughout all of this, I continued to help the women at Alderson with their cases, listening to their stories. Having spent so much time with them over the years, I realized how many of them—unable to afford expensive legal representation—were appointed federal public defenders instead. Public defenders who sometimes fell far short of what these women needed. I heard women talk about all the things their attorneys didn't do; what they wished they would have done. I listened to stories about how they felt forced into pleading guilty, or not listened to, or ignored entirely. Women whose cases had been neglected for months or hadn't been investigated as they had asked.

I thought about these stories—and then I thought about Peter. Peter, who, at every step, in every way, had set the bar in terms of what attorneys are supposed to do for their clients. It wasn't lost on me how fortunate I was that my family could pull together the funds to hire him for my initial trial. But it also wasn't lost on me how inherently unfair even that reality was. Especially when considering the fact that a disproportionate number of low-income people enter the prison system year after year—people who cannot afford to hire private attorneys—and most of them are Black and brown. A person's income or finances should never dictate the level of legal representation they receive. But it too often does. And clearly, from the huge numbers of poor Black and brown people filling the federal prison system, there are real and dangerous consequences as a result.

With every woman I listened to at Alderson, my career path became clearer. I didn't want people to go through what these women had endured under a system that completely failed them—as it had failed me. When I became a lawyer, I wanted to provide people with a different experience if I could. I wanted to protect people's rights in the way they were meant to be protected and to be able to give people the same level of representation Peter had given to me, whether they could pay $5 for it or $50,000.

It was there, in prison, through talking and listening to the rest of the women in the compound, and realizing just how messed up this system was, that I knew that I wanted to become a public defender.

When my second appeal was denied in October 2006, the outcome didn't discourage me, not like it had the first time around. I had less than two months left on the sentence anyway—and my momentum couldn't be broken. I was already thinking forward, looking ahead. Mentally preparing for my life on the other side.

CHAPTER 17

DURING YOUR LAST STRETCH OF TIME INSIDE, ALDERSON REQUIRES EVERY soon-departing resident to go through a prerelease program aimed to ease the reentry process into society. The classes, largely focused on navigating the job market—finding work, keeping work—were supposed to give us the skills we needed to pave the way for our success on the outside. They were supposed to help get us on our feet, after years of being locked away. Except, after entering the prelease program, I quickly became convinced that these classes were deliberately designed to do the opposite.

During one class, a temp agency came onto the compound to teach us how to write up our résumés. Many of the women at Alderson had been locked up for six, seven, sometimes even ten-plus years. We knew any kind of traditional résumé would only work against us, as it would draw attention to those often huge gaps in time—an automatic disqualifier for many potential employers. But instead of providing us alternatives that might give us a fairer shot, chronological résumés were the only ones taught, the only ones talked about. It was like they were setting us up for failure from the outset.

And so, slowly, a group of us started stepping in as best we could to fill the obvious void in the quality of reentry education. We started talking about what we might do to construct résumés differently—how we might organize them to better keep us in a game that was already rigged against anyone with a criminal record. And then, we began writing these résumés for ourselves and for other women at Alderson who were soon up for release. We worked together to organize them functionally instead—emphasizing mastery of skills and roles rather than listing work experience chronologically—and gave these documents to the women to use when they got out.

We did whatever we could for each other to put ourselves in a better position on the other side. Because we knew that the barriers out there existed—ones that too many people would find impossible to get over, to get around, to pass underneath.

I would take this lesson with me in the months to come.

———

BECAUSE THERE IS NO PAROLE IN THE FEDERAL SYSTEM, INCARCERATED people are required to serve a minimum of 85 percent of their sentence before becoming eligible for release. And so, as the year came to a close, I got word that after serving three years and ten months at Alderson—85 percent of my five-year mandatory minimum, plus the additional time knocked off for good behavior—I would finally be eligible for release.

On December 1, 2006, I would be going home.

As I prepared to leave on the eve of my release, the emotions were bittersweet. I would be starting a new chapter but leaving behind deep and meaningful friendships. I thought about the tradition so many of the women at Alderson participated in before they left. On Sundays during service in the chapel, if you put in a request with Chaplain Walker, she would get out her guitar and sing a song she wrote, called the "Pocket Song." I don't know where or how the tradition began, but it was something Chaplain Walker had become known for over the years: "I'm gonna take you with me, wherever I go," she sang, whenever it was one of our times to go. "'Cuz I could never leave, never could leave you behind. I'll slip you into my, slip you into my pocket. For you know I'm never gonna let you go."

On my last Sunday at Alderson, as Chaplain Walker sang the "Pocket Song," her words were a reminder of all of the friendships, all of the stories, I would carry with me forever.

On my last night at Alderson, I passed between my friends' cubes one final time—shedding tears, giving hugs, collecting contacts. I said goodbye to the women who'd gotten me through the last few years—

Sylvia and Peaches, Gina and Syreeta, Kila and Strawberry, and so, so many others. For a second time, I gave away the last few items I'd accumulated over the course of my time living in the compound. Things I knew I would no longer need. But this time, when I passed through Alderson's gates, I was certain there would be no coming back.

Crawling into bed that evening, I didn't sleep at all. I sat up on my top bunk and literally watched the clock—counting down the seconds, the minutes, the hours. And after I heard the early morning whistle blow, I gathered my things and walked down the hill with a few friends who wanted to see me off, making my way to the same R&D building I had walked into almost four years prior. This time, however, I prepared to go home.

I was given the option of traveling home on a Greyhound bus, paid for by the prison. It was a "courtesy" Alderson offered all of the inmates upon their release. An infuriating gesture, considering the many hours we all spent doing often backbreaking work around the compound, making less than a dollar per day. I had declined the offer in the release plan we were made to write for the prison, which detailed where we were going to live once we were let out, and how we were going to get there. I was thankful that my parents had agreed to send me a one-way plane ticket to Nashville instead.

I changed into a new outfit my family had sent me—a gold-and-black–striped turtleneck, black jeans, and boots. Putting on my own clothes, I realized that I would never have to wear my khaki prison uniform ever again.

Then, I was driven out of the gates of Alderson one last time, bound for the airport in Beckley. But this time, I would not be handcuffed and shackled on the ride there. I wouldn't be escorted on board a plane flanked by US Marshals carrying guns pointing directly at me or shuttled afterward from one dirty, overcrowded facility to the next.

This time, when I boarded the plane—for only the second time in my life—I would be doing it as a free woman. I was twenty-eight years old.

———

THE AIRPORT IN BECKLEY WAS TINY, WHICH MEANT THAT DIRECT flights anywhere were impossible to come by. Instead, you typically had to hop on a small plane to the nearest bigger city along your way, then continue your travels from there. The morning I left Alderson, the sky was dark and overcast, and a storm threatened to unleash from the clouds. I walked onto the little twin-engine jet feeling nervous, hoping the weather would hold. But when we began to ascend during takeoff, the entire cabin shook as we dipped and swerved, hitting pockets of rough air. To say the flight was bad would be an understatement. We were thrown around in the skies the entire time—my stomach churning with every sudden drop. *I'm finally leaving prison*, I thought, squeezing the armrests on either side of me. *And now I'm going to die on this airplane.*

When we finally touched down in Pittsburgh for my connection hours later, I thanked God that I was alive. Then, I promptly searched the airport for some Dramamine.

Walking through the airport to the gate for my connecting flight, I took in all of the sights and sounds. There was black and gold everywhere—the official colors of the Pittsburgh Steelers. Weaving through the hustle and bustle around me, I began to fully grasp the fact that I was no longer property of Alderson. Given the turbulence of my previous flight, it was the first time that I could begin to let that reality sink in.

I walked into one of the little convenience stores, finding the Dramamine and adding gum and snacks to my pile at the checkout counter. I hadn't breathed fresh air or had real food in almost four years. Later, seated at the gate, I had to fight back tears—because, yes, I was finally free.

The rest of the trip went much more smoothly. From Pittsburgh I flew to North Carolina, where we switched crews on the plane, then made our final leg to Nashville. Looking out of my window from thirty thousand feet in the now calm air, seeing the wide expanse of clouds and earth and green below, I finally let myself breathe a little easier. I thought about the women at Alderson I was leaving behind. The people who had been my most immediate support system over these last few years. We kept each other going. We encouraged each other. For many of us, we were all that we had. If God had a bigger plan for me, certainly the impact of these women was part of it. I vowed that I would take their stories with me, keeping them in my pocket, and use them as motivation for whatever was to come.

———

ONCE I ARRIVED AT THE AIRPORT IN NASHVILLE, I WAS GREETED BY A small group of friends and relatives who were all waiting for me. My parents and brothers were there, along with Pinky and my aunt Shawn. Anitra would have been there too, if she still lived in town. During the course of my trial, Anitra had gotten married and moved to Mississippi with her football coach husband and their daughter. Her case, in the end, was settled after she took a plea deal, which gave her probation but thankfully no time to serve. After all the drama of the last few years, my sister was ready for a fresh start, and I didn't blame her.

Everyone gathered at that airport in Nashville had rallied around me, always. Supported me, always, during these last few years of trials and disappointments, wins and losses. But I don't remember a lot about this long-anticipated reunion. I know that it was over-whelming to see so many people I was forced to love from afar for so long, now suddenly so up close. I know I felt the typical emotions you might expect: happiness, joy, relief. But for me, the entire thing was also overshadowed by another pressing reality. I couldn't finally go home with my family, to sleep in my own bed, under my own sheets. Because as soon as I touched down in Nashville, the timer was set again. If I didn't soon report to the halfway house where I was made to stay immediately after my release—the first stop for everyone who leaves prison—I would be marked as an escapee. So, I rushed through hugs and hellos, then my parents and Pinky packed up my things in their car and made the fifteen-minute drive to Diersen Charities, my home for the next six months.

The halfway house staff was waiting when I got there to check me in, then I was pointed toward a bed in a big, open room that made up the women's living quarters. The facility was co-ed, split into two separate sleeping areas for men and women, with eight to twelve beds in the women's section, and many more—at least twenty—in the men's. In these spaces, the men always outnumbered the women.

I unpacked my few belongings and prepared once again to spend my first night in a new place, sleeping next to strangers. This was not the end of my prison life; I was simply moving into the next evolution: from incarcerated to formerly incarcerated. Free, but not free. A new chapter was beginning with a whole new set of challenges to navigate and learn from.

chapter 18

OVER AND OVER AGAIN, THE IMPORTANCE OF EMPLOYMENT WAS stressed to the residents of the halfway house by the staff, when we first checked in. Jobs were currency; they allowed you to move more freely outside the house. Get a job and you could be granted a pass to leave the facility for an hour to go to, say, Walmart if you needed to pick up a few things. Keep a job for a certain period of time and you could be granted a day pass, or an overnight pass, or a weekend pass to see your family. And eventually, after you held onto one for long enough, you could transition to home confinement, moving out of the halfway house altogether. The quicker you got a job, the quicker you could move through the system and earn more privileges. And—most importantly—the quicker you could pay the facility the 25 percent of your paycheck that it was entitled to receive. Once residents moved into Phase 1 of the halfway house system—securing employment—the rules stipulated that we had to fork over this percentage of our salaries to cover room and board. This was the real reason they wanted us to get a job so quickly. This payment—or "subsistence" as it was called—was what allowed many of these facilities to stay afloat.

Employment, for many within the formerly incarcerated community, is a *huge* barrier to reentry. People who want to support themselves and their families, who are eager to join the workforce, are often hindered because their convictions serve as the ultimate scarlet letter throughout the process. Studies show that more than one out of four formerly incarcerated people looking for work cannot find a job. The unemployment rates for these communities are nearly five times higher than they are for the general population, despite the data that people with convictions are more active in their job searches than their peers without the stigma of a criminal record.

Not surprisingly, within these numbers, formerly incarcerated people of color bear the brunt of the discrimination, preventing access to the jobs we need to survive. The unemployment rate for formerly incarcerated Black men? 35.0 percent—compared to 18.4 percent of white men in the same community. And the rates for Black women who are formerly incarcerated? 43 percent—compared to 23 percent of white women—*double* that of their white women counterparts. Line for line, the hierarchy of systemic inequality is on full display: People of color are worse off than whites; women fare worse than men; and Black women are the most disenfranchised of all.

Knowing this context now, it is not lost on me how fortunate I was. Unlike so many people in my community, leaving prison, I had a job to walk into. And not just any job—one that could serve as a significant entry point to my career.

Three days after I returned home from Alderson, I started working in Peter's office as his law clerk. I did this without having to worry about a background check; without the anxiety of having to explain my prison history or having to go through many of the standard reentry procedures that block otherwise qualified candidates from getting jobs. And I did it knowing the privilege my education had afforded me—I understood that my college degree from TSU increased my chances of securing a job and earning more than minimum wage.

Once I'd confirmed my position at Peter's law firm, I was able to move into Phase 1 of the halfway house system, which allowed me to leave, but only to go to work and come home. Every day, I checked out at the front desk, then walked straight down Eighth Avenue to Peter's office—at which point I had to call the halfway house again to announce that I had arrived. I had never used public transportation before—it didn't exist in Franklin while I was growing up—so trying to figure out Nashville's bus system was completely new to me. Even the time I'd spent in Nashville while I was at TSU for college, I was still just commuting back and forth from Franklin. This would be my first time actually living in Nashville. It was a lot to try to figure out the ins and outs of the transportation for the city, in addition to everything else I was navigating now in my new world. Plus, I didn't yet have my car—this was another privilege you had to earn your way up to at the halfway house. So, I took to the streets instead, learning Nashville as best as I could on foot, starting with my walk to work.

After spending so much time walking only through the compound at Alderson, I was finally free to walk wherever I wanted to walk, go wherever I wanted to go—however I chose to get there. I made it a point to take different routes to get to Peter's office, enjoying my various surroundings. It was December when I began this new routine, but walking in the cold was nothing for me after experiencing three years of West Virginia winters. I would take the bus whenever it got too cold, but I always preferred to walk instead, to experience that kind of small freedom. My family bought me a brand-new pair of white Reeboks that I would put on every morning before I headed out the door.

As Peter's law clerk, I started out doing mostly legal research. Peter handled both state and federal cases, and I worked on a lot of them. Whatever Peter needed me to do, I did. Some days that meant spending hours going through mountains of discovery, categorizing what I found. Other days I would listen to electronically monitored phone calls and take notes on what was said. I grew to be Peter's right hand—searching for any holes in the cases we could use to our advantage to benefit his clients. Any possible ways we could file motions on their behalf or find just the right case law to use to petition the courts to give them less time. After so many years working together on my own case doing similar research—looking into what could possibly be done to craft a more successful argument—the job felt like a familiar continuation. As soon as I came on board, it was like we fell into step, right back into our old routine. But now, of course, the circumstances couldn't have been more different.

I was getting paid $25 an hour, working forty hours a week, which was a phenomenal amount compared to the salaries of most of the people coming off often long sentences. Many of those in my community had no choice but to work low-wage jobs in light of the stigma around their criminal convictions. Being forced to pay the halfway house that 25 percent subsistence out of their salaries on top of that, every single month, often left little to survive on. And even if you do manage to keep steady work and make the subsistence payments on time, consequently earning the privilege to move out of the halfway house and into home confinement—that 25 percent still needs to be paid until your six months under their thumb is up. Meaning, you were paying for room and board at a facility you were no longer using because you'd done what you were supposed to do by moving out and finding permanent housing. It was not uncommon for up to three different people to be paying their 25 percent for the same unused bed.

This is the contradiction of the system—one of the many, many ways it is constructed with the explicit intent of working against the people who are put through it. The purpose of reentry facilities like halfway houses, on the surface, is to help formerly incarcerated people get on their feet in those first six months after release. They are there to help them find employment so they can become financially stable and independent. They are there to encourage them to find housing so people can start building up their lives. But baked into the structure of these very same facilities are barriers that make it difficult for formerly incarcerated people to reach the milestones they "want" for us. The longer I spent there, the more it became clear to me that the halfway house system was nothing more than a money-making scheme.

————

ABOUT THREE MONTHS INTO MY STAY AT THE FACILITY, I HAD MOVED through the different phases and earned enough privileges to transition to home confinement. While searching through the "For Rent" ads one day, I found a duplex apartment in Nashville available for $500/month. I called the number listed and talked to the landlady, telling her that I was interested. I mentioned that I was a law clerk at a local firm and that my grandmother was happy to cosign for the apartment for me, if necessary. Though I was prepared for a full inquest into my past, she didn't ask for my criminal history; she didn't even do a background check. I simply gave her copies of my pay stubs and printed off a copy of my credit report for her records. And even though she never asked, I told her about my situation anyway, but she just waved it away. She liked me and she liked Pinky too, as does everybody who meets her. Seeing my check stubs, she knew that I had the ability to pay rent on time, and she believed that I would take good care of the apartment. For her, that was enough. And so, within a week or so after I first met with my landlady, I secured the duplex—paid for entirely with the money I earned myself, working for Peter. Then, I began the process of getting approved by the halfway house to move in.

I was one of the lucky ones. I heard so many stories—from the people I was meeting at the halfway house, from my friends at Alderson who were also now released—about the enormous difficulties they faced trying to get housing. So many people were automatically turned down because of background checks. Others had to take themselves out of the running because many places, especially at apartment complexes, required steep security deposits up-front, with zero flexibility on the payments. And when you're using earnings from a job that doesn't pay nearly what you need, to pay out that 25 percent subsistence at the halfway house—along with taking care of phone bills, and utility bills, and providing for family—money gets gone real quick. Fall behind in one area, and it's often a domino effect to the bottom, with no one standing by to support you if you fall. Formerly incarcerated people are routinely denied public housing assistance. We are almost ten times more likely to be homeless than the general public. And once we do fall into homelessness, we are far more likely to be incarcerated again.

Thus, the revolving door of the criminal justice system continues.

The chance Peter gave me, the one my new landlady was giving me—even my grandmother's willingness to act as my cosigner if I needed it—these things are all emblematic of the kind of culture that formerly incarcerated people need to thrive. A culture of acceptance. A culture where people are seen for who they are, not for what they've done. A culture that allows us the same amount of space and grace as everyone else to grow into who we want to become.

chapter 19

A S I SETTLED INTO LIFE IN MY DUPLEX, I TURNED MY ATTENTION again to law school. I started taking classes to prepare for the LSAT, studying between my workday at Peter's office. After months and months of grinding out full workdays, on top of long nights studying, I was finally ready to take the test. I passed and immediately turned my attention to applying to law school. Around this time, I also began a master's program in criminology. *You can never have too many options,* I thought to myself. And I didn't have any time left to lose.

The University of Florida had long been my dream, ever since I shared my plans with Professor Woods in college all those years ago. But I had lost four years of my life since then. I was bound, in Nashville, to some form of supervised release for the next five years. And my support system was in and around Nashville too. My family and friends in nearby Franklin, my job at Peter's office. And so, I did some research, and in 2008, I officially enrolled in the Nashville School of Law (NSL), an institution designed to accommodate people who wanted to pursue their degrees while continuing their full-time employment.

Twice a week, I went to my law school classes at night after full days spent in Peter's office. In between—somehow—I kept chipping away at my master's. I would also be paying for law school out of pocket; so, to supplement my income, after my first year, I started working in NSL's library. Two jobs. Two school programs. On top of the day-to-day demands to stay on top of the conditions of my release.

And, of course, the people in charge of managing my supervision didn't make things any easier for me. "You're never going to be able to do both of these things at the same time," my supervise release officer constantly told me. "Why are you even trying?"

When I first started my position with Peter at the firm, rather than being supportive of this accomplishment, the supervise release officer I was assigned to questioned how I managed to get it. When I first moved into my duplex, she'd stop by frequently—always unannounced—wanting to search in my closets and drawers, looking for drugs or any illegal activity. Walking into my room, she'd check underneath my bed or in the closets, looking for any other formerly incarcerated person I might be hiding there, to ensure I was complying with the no-contact rule.

The system was filled with people like her—gatekeepers who were looking for any reason to lock people back up, rather than working to ensure people made successful transitions back into society. Those who were more interested in the punitive aspect of the criminal justice system than in the rehabilitative aspect.

Over the years, pushing forward in spite of people's lack of support or belief in me became a kind of norm. At every step, when I shared my plans, there were those who offered their skepticism freely. Some doubted whether I could appeal my conviction. Others doubted if I could complete law school or whether I would be able to practice law at all with a felony on my record.

But, luckily for me, there were also people who saw beyond the potential obstacles. And instead of sharing their skepticism, they extended their help and support.

Shortly after I applied to NSL, I met with the school's associate dean, Virginia Townzen. I wanted to talk with her about my situation, to let her know what was going on so she would have a heads-up from the outset. I remember sitting down in her office, going through the details of my case: the unfair conviction, the time spent in Alderson fighting for my appeal, and my desire to pursue a career in law throughout.

"Okay," she responded after I'd finished, unruffled by the information I'd just laid out before her. "Here's what you should do."

Occupational licensing boards remain a significant problem for people who have been formerly incarcerated. They can reject applications outright from anyone with a felony conviction. Tennessee is one of the harsher regulatory states in this respect, ranked thirteenth in the country. In Tennessee there are 110 types of jobs that require a license, and nearly every board can deny you one due to past crimes, even misdemeanors. Of course, practicing law is one of those professions requiring a license. Dean Townzen knew the hoops I would have to jump through to obtain my law license. To be able to even take the bar after I graduated from law school, I had to submit an application that outlined my entire history over the past ten years, which would then be evaluated by the Tennessee Board of Law Examiners to determine whether I had the character and fitness to become a lawyer.

"Because of your record," Dean Townzen explained, "determining whether you have the moral character to practice is going to be your biggest hurdle." But there were things I could do now, she said, to be ready for the board's challenges when the time came to submit my application. "They might want you to see a therapist, or—because your conviction involves drugs—they may ask you to provide documentation that you don't have any substance abuse issues." She referred me to an assistance program for people in the legal profession that provided free counseling and drug testing. "Go see a therapist; do whatever evaluations you might need to do," Dean Townzen told me. "Take care of these things on the front end, to give them less of an opportunity to deny you." One by one, she ticked off each of my potential setbacks and then gave me a game plan to overcome them. Here was someone who clearly wanted me to succeed. Here was someone committed to giving me the second chance the system had repeatedly denied me.

———

I TOOK DEAN TOWNZEN'S ADVICE AND REACHED OUT TO THE HEAD OF the program she'd mentioned during our meeting, who then referred me to a therapist. I set a time to see her, prepared to do whatever needed to be done.

I have always been a big proponent of therapy. A lot of people, especially in the Black community, want to say that Black folks don't go to therapy—we do, and we should. Especially when it comes to formerly incarcerated people reentering society, it is one of the many missing key components when it comes to making a successful transition.

My own time inside the criminal justice system showed me just how deeply traumatizing it can be. People lost loved ones. They missed important moments with their families. They experienced violence inside prison, and so many other things that make incarceration—hell, the criminal justice system as a whole—traumatic.

You can learn to suppress that trauma, but it doesn't go away; it just gets buried deeper. And then, when it's time to reenter society and finally process it, you often don't know how. How can you be expected to, when you've shut that part of you down for so long? On top of dealing with things like these, there's also having to deal with the scarlet "F"—for felon—you now have on your chest, and everything that comes along with that: The judgment you're going to be faced with. The pressure of trying to be successful according to *whoever's* standards of success. The pressures of having a job, reconnecting with family, finding housing, and assimilating to a new "normal."

Adding in the complicated layer of being involved in the criminal justice system, and everything that comes along with that, the picture can often look overwhelming very quickly. But therapy is rarely offered as a component of reentry, and the implications of this are huge. Without a way to address mental health, many formerly incarcerated people are denied the opportunity to truly heal. We're denied the possibility of trying to become whole again.

Sitting in those sessions with my therapist—talking about the struggles, the setbacks, the how's and the why's—I realized just how much self-reflection work really began for me at Alderson. I learned not to reject the parts of me that had been judged as "negative," but to take them back and redefine them.

Learning to own every part of me meant owning my conviction as well. That, too, was a part of me, but it didn't have to define any aspect of who I was.

After my sessions had ended, the therapist wrote me a letter, attesting to my moral character. *Keeda Haynes is more than fit to be a licensed practicing attorney in the state of Tennessee,* she wrote. I stuck the letter into a folder and saved it for my bar application.

chapter 20

Life moved forward. I juggled school and work, both at
Peter's office and at NSL's law library.

After a full year of doing my master's program and law school
simultaneously, I realized something had to give. Law school would
only ramp up further from here on out. So, I decided to end my master's early, with only one semester left to finish. I was disappointed
but also focused, more than ever, on being ruthless with my time in
service of my larger goal to practice law. And so, I pressed on—trying
to keep pace with my busy schedule, on top of continuing to adjust
to new day-to-day routines that didn't revolve around Count Times
or whistles—finding new ways of staying grounded.

Shortly after I moved to Nashville, I began attending Mount
Zion Baptist Church, a place that had been rooted in the town's
Black community for centuries. One Sunday, I saw on the program
that they were having a meeting for their prison ministry, and I
decided that I wanted to go and check it out.

Mount Zion's prison ministry was focused primarily on going
into jails and doing Bible studies, or preaching, or simply praying

for people. The support they offered was geared toward a person's time *inside* prison, but I realized from my own experiences that people needed just as much support—maybe even more so—once they were released.

After some time being involved in the ministry, building relationships with many families impacted by incarceration in our local community, I began talking with Joe Ravenell, one of the ministry's leaders, about some additional ways we might consider approaching our work. It was true that too often people with convictions are released into cities whose programs and policies—and very infrastructure—are built against their best interests. Discriminatory hiring practices and housing policies and a whole host of other barriers prevented formerly incarcerated people from accessing goals they wanted and needed to reach.

But before even facing these larger barriers to reentry, I also knew that people coming out of jails and prisons were not given even the basics. Many go back into society with no driver's licenses, no birth certificates or social security cards; without basic necessities like socks and underwear. All of those essentials that people forget about when they talk about reentry. Without an ID, applying for jobs, housing, and social services is nearly impossible. But to get an ID, you need a copy of your birth certificate and a social security card—which cost money, depleting funds that are already in short supply.

I knew that before people exiting the system could even begin tackling those larger barriers to reentry—finding housing, getting employment—many needed help meeting their most basic needs. That, I thought, was where our prison ministry could come in: asking people what those needs were, then providing ways to meet them. To be truly helpful, we needed to listen and meet people exactly where they were.

Mr. Ravenell was open to the idea and allowed me to create a new component of the church's prison ministry that specifically focused on this aspect of reentry. I began working with Chanel, another woman involved with the prison ministry, to create a survey that would identify the specific, individual needs of formerly incarcerated people in our area. We started, at first, in halfway houses, where there's not much support for people coming out of the local state facilities. There, we handed out our surveys, asking the men and women residents to fill them out. Some people told us they needed personal items—soap, toothbrushes and toothpaste, underwear and socks. Some people needed leads for jobs. Others needed help obtaining those government-issued IDs or driver's licenses so they could begin the job search process.

Looking through the results of the surveys reconfirmed what I already knew: there was no one-size-fits-all concept of success when it came to reentry. There was no standard twelve-step program that the hundreds of thousands of people coming out of prisons each year could possibly fit into. I knew that because the system negatively impacted different communities in diverse ways, there simply could not be just one standard starting point. But I knew that if we didn't start with meeting people's basic needs—whatever those needs were—we would not be able to help effectively.

After starting with one halfway house, we moved on to others—gathering information from the facilities' residents, then taking it back to the church to brainstorm resources, support, and supplies. To further our work, Mr. Ravenell came up with the idea of doing a series of informational events at the halfway houses called "Community Talks" to help with reentry. Drawing from my days of helping the women at Alderson, I went to different facilities discussing résumé writing and also added in some information about interviewing skills. We had people come in and talk about the basics of money management—how to open a bank account, how to write checks. And we would invite people from the church who worked in different fields—in education or finance or social services—to be part of the Community Talks as well, sharing with people at the facilities whatever specialized knowledge they had.

Through this work with Mount Zion, I was embodying the second-chance culture I wanted to see around me. I thought about my own community. People in my life like my family, and Peter and Dean Townzen, who were invested in my success. *Everyone going through reentry should have access to this kind of support,* I thought, regardless of whether it came from their own personal networks or not. The same kind of second-chance culture—that deep, sustained investment—that I received, day in, day out, from the people around me who never stopped helping along my way.

———

SOON AFTER I JOINED THE PRISON MINISTRY AT MOUNT ZION IN 2008, I petitioned Judge Trauger to end my probation early. I was enrolled in law school; I had done enough work to almost complete a master's, and I was still working for Peter—a position I obtained within days of getting out—alongside picking up the extra income by working in the library. Surely, this was proof enough that I was taking productive steps to make the best of my life since I'd been released.

But when Peter filed the motion, Sunny Koshy sent back a swift rebuttal, arguing that I shouldn't be rewarded for doing what I was supposed to do. And when the paperwork eventually got into the hands of Judge Trauger, she promptly denied the request, stating, *It's too early for Ms. Haynes to be released from her supervised release.*

Judge Trauger's decision to keep me under supervision meant, among so many other things, that I still could not legally cast my vote. Unlike the two states that allowed voting rights to be restored immediately after release from prison, Tennessee laws said that people convicted of felony crimes could only regain their voting rights after they'd successfully completed probation. Tennessee is the only state that not only requires you to have paid off all court fines, fees, and restitution but also to be up-to-date on child support before you can gain voter restoration. Because of Judge Trauger's decision, I would not be eligible to get my voting rights reinstated for another two years.

This was in 2008. It meant that while much of the country was voting for our first Black president, I—along with thousands of other formerly incarcerated people affected by restrictive voting laws in Tennessee—was left out of this historic moment. Excluded from the opportunity to participate in the excitement and jubilation of an event—the first one of its kind—that I will never, ever be able to reclaim.

It reminded me of so many things the system takes from you— memories, experiences, freedoms—that it can never truly give back.

According to a October 2020 report created by the Sentencing Project, there are over five million people in this country who cannot vote because of a felony conviction. And, not surprisingly, these numbers disproportionately impact communities of color—Black people, very specifically. African Americans of voting age are nearly four times as likely to lose their voting rights than the rest of the adult population, with one out of every sixteen Black adults disenfranchised nationally.

Voter disenfranchisement at the hands of the government, especially where Black communities are concerned, is nothing new. It is a story as old as Reconstruction, when white-controlled America— incensed that the race they'd enslaved for centuries was suddenly enfranchised in the wake of Emancipation in 1865—formed lynch mobs to brutally murder and terrorize us out of exercising our right to vote. The Ku Klux Klan rose out of white resentment and fears about Black voting power, with many local government officials, disguised under white hoods and robes, leading the charge in our torture and deaths.

In the decades that followed, state legislatures across the country passed new laws, constitutions, and amendments that made voter registration and voting more difficult for Black people. They based their voting requirements on conditions they knew many Black people could not meet because the country had historically robbed them of those abilities. There were expensive poll taxes Black people could not pay. Literacy tests they could not pass because, of course, for centuries educating Black people in many parts of the country was illegal. In New York, for a time, the government even required that Black people provide proof of property ownership before they allowed us into the voting booth.

Today, over a million Black Americans are banned from voting. In Tennessee alone, more than 20 percent of Black American adults of voting age—more than one in five—are disenfranchised. It's one of only four states where more than 8 percent of the adult population is disenfranchised.

Paired with extreme voting rules that make Tennessee the third-hardest state for voter participation, this adds up to mass disenfranchisement that protects the status quo but leaves Tennessee's most vulnerable people with little opportunity to make our voices heard in the voting booth.

I was one of those silenced numbers until 2010, when I was finally eligible to get my voting rights restored. Two years after her initial denial, at last, Judge Trauger agreed to release me from supervision. I had been in law school for two whole years before they thought that I had done enough, proved myself enough, to be released early.

CHAPTER 20

I was finally done with the punitive aspect of my situation. No more calls to check in, no more asking for permission to go out of state, no more supervisors popping up at my house at random hours. But even with this milestone, I knew I would never, ever truly be free. The system could not make up for all those years lost. It couldn't return me to the person I was before. And it couldn't erase the stigma that I, and so many other formerly incarcerated people, were forced to carry with us. The label as a felon—that scarlet "F"—forever emblazoned across your chest. Even when it was done with you, the system would continue to leave you reminders of where you'd been. Or what freedoms and rights it could still try to deny you.

I was able to vote for Barack Obama's reelection in 2012. And it felt good to finally be a part of the democratic process. To have a voice in the issues that mattered to me and to my community. But the feeling wasn't the same. Another experience can never make up for the one you've missed. The first Black president had already been elected. The historic moment had passed. That's the thing about time: there's just no getting it back.

chapter 21

As I approached my final stretch of law school, I began narrowing my focus on the future.

My desire to work in the Public Defender's Office hadn't wavered since I first came to the decision at Alderson. Being involved in the prison ministry at Mount Zion and moving through the process of reentry myself had only solidified the decision for me. With so much wrong with the system—with so much corruption—I was convinced that my role was to represent those who suffered the same injustices I did, and to dismantle the system. To correct the imbalance as best as I could, with whatever bit of power I could wield from my position. The Public Defender's Office was where I needed to be.

One of my law professors was also an assistant public defender in the Nashville office, and I did an internship with her. When I wasn't in class or working in Peter's office, I met her at the courthouse downtown, taking the elevators to the sixth floor, to the courtroom of Judge Norman, the Criminal Court, Division IV judge. There, I shadowed my professor on the job, watching as she met with clients and moved through her caseload.

Around the same time, I learned that one of the local bar associations was having a job fair. I signed up to be considered for an interview with the Public Defender's Office—and with that office only. I knew, at that point, that I didn't want to begin my career anywhere else. I got notice that they were interested in me too, and when I arrived at the fair, I was interviewed by two attorneys at the office. We talked through my résumé and my background, and why I wanted to enter the office. They were currently on a hiring freeze, they told me, but said they would definitely keep my information on file and also pass it along to Dawn Deaner, the chief public defender at the time. Sometime later, I did receive an email from Dawn Deaner, thanking me for my interest and telling me again that they were on a hiring freeze but to keep checking back. And so, from that point on, that's exactly what I did. Every six months or so, I sent her a quick email to keep me at the top of her mind.

The months flew by, drawing nearer and nearer to graduation day. Two months before I was scheduled to finish up my last classes and cross the stage, I had to submit my bar application. This would be the first big, official hurdle to cross. The one Dean Townzen warned me about when we first sat together in her office, strategizing about how to convince the Tennessee Board of Law Examiners that I was qualified to become an attorney—even with a felony conviction on my record.

They wanted a comprehensive paper trail of your life: where you lived; where you worked; your credit history; and, of course, your criminal background. Gathering up my documents, I included the note from my therapist attesting to my character, along with a detailed summary of everything involved in my case. The application quickly ballooned into an entire binder's worth of material: the indictment, the judgment, presentence reports, my appeals process—I gave them everything. Probably more than they needed or cared to look through. But I didn't want to give them any reason to think I had something to hide.

A month or so later, I got a call to set up my character and fitness interview with Shelton Anderson, a local defense attorney. It was his job to give a recommendation about whether I had the character and fitness to sit for the bar exam in the state of Tennessee.

On the day of our interview, my binder sat open on the table between us as he paged through the last few years of my life. All of the trials, all of the tribulations, all of the hard-earned wins and disappointing losses were there, on full display. We talked about my interests—my studies during law school, my desire to become a public defender—before he arrived at the moment we'd both been warming up for.

"I'm not going to lie, your background is a concern," Shelton told me, without any malice in his voice. "I really don't think they're going to let you practice." I knew that even if I was allowed to take the bar, and passed, the Tennessee Board of Law Examiners could still request that I jump through an additional hoop, in the form of what's called a Show-Cause hearing. It would be another round of proving my character and fitness to practice law all over again—this time before a panel from the Tennessee Board of Law Examiners.

"I'm going to recommend that you take the bar anyway," he added. "But like I said, I don't think they'll admit you."

He delivered his assessment more like he was stating the facts rather than passing judgment. Like he was doing me a favor by preparing me for what was to come. I hadn't even graduated from law school yet, and I was being told that my dreams were likely a dead end.

But, nonetheless, he was recommending that I take the bar. That's all that mattered.

———

THAT SPRING OF 2012—AFTER FOUR YEARS OF HARD WORK, I OFFI-cially graduated from the Nashville School of Law with my JD. Hold-ing that diploma in my hands felt like a blessing. Reading my name in print—*Keeda Jarresse Haynes, Doctor of Jurisprudence*—I took in the gravity of the words. I knew that this moment was over a decade in the making. A dream I had steadily, relentlessly moved toward ever since I realized what I wanted to do while taking Professor Woods's Legal Methods class. I knew this moment was important. And I genuinely celebrated the achievement with family and friends: I smiled while they cheered for me in the audience; we hugged and toasted to the occasion during a brunch afterward. But as with every other milestone in the last decade—graduating from college, winning my appeal, finally being released from prison—I also knew the achieve-ment was accompanied by an equally important "but." Another looming hurdle to cross. Another potential barrier that threatened to erode all of the progress I'd made so far. In this way, I'd come to regard these big, important milestones not like I was crossing some sort of finish line, but like I'd made it to another rest stop along a marathon. They were moments to catch my breath and refocus be-fore hitting the pavement again.

Next stop: bar exam—and then the Show-Cause hearing that might follow.

I continued to work full-time while I studied throughout that summer and took all of July off from work at Peter's office to prepare to take the exam at the end of the month. Each day I studied steadily for ten hours, taking a few fifteen- or thirty-minute breaks to eat or drink and rest my eyes, but, for the most part, that ten-hour-a-day routine went uninterrupted. It was all bar exam prep, all the time.

The day I went in to take the exam, I walked through the front doors of the testing site, thinking that I was as prepared as I was ever going to be.

CHAPTER 21

The exam would be administered over the next two days. After that, there would be three months of waiting until the results posted. After I submitted the last of my materials to the proctor and exited the building for the last time, I felt, at least, that I knew *something*. I was confident in the answers I knew and tried to block out any of the ones I felt less sure of. People often say that no one ever truly knows when they walk out of the bar exam how they did. I had done everything I could have. Whether it was enough to pass, we'd just have to wait and see.

During these months of limbo, I kept myself busy—continuing to work for Peter; staying involved in the prison ministry at Mount Zion; trying to carry on with my life as best I could, knowing so much was riding on these results. I also checked in with Dawn Deaner in the Public Defender's Office, letting her know that I'd just taken the bar and remained just as interested as ever in working there. "Great— let's talk again after you hear back about the exam," she wrote me in response. Dawn was also thinking about the possibility of the Show-Cause hearing, even if the results of the test did go my way. It seemed like everything in my future hinged on whatever came next—on the other side of this three-month wait.

Finally, that October, the day had come when the results would be posted online. I got on and off the phone with a couple of my classmates as we waited for the results to post. Mostly I talked to a classmate of mine named Heather, who lived in a rural part of town with unreliable, slow internet. She and I sat in front of our respective computers, constantly clicking the "refresh" button on the website. We refreshed, and refreshed, and refreshed again, watching our screens for any sign of change. And then, after what seemed like a lifetime, the results finally came up. I made my way down the list of names, scrolling past the "E's," the "F's," the "G's"—until I reached H. *Hancock . . . Harvey . . . Hathaway.*

And then, there it was: Haynes.

I had passed. *Thank you, Lord.* I had made it through—and on the first try.

I was excited to be one step closer. But, of course, there would be another period of "wait and see." I hoped that passing the bar would be the end of it; that now I could finally just get on with my career. I hoped that a notice about going through a Show-Cause hearing would never come. That maybe the board would determine that everything I'd achieved so far was enough. I wanted them to say that I had sufficiently proven myself; that my conviction didn't have to be another roadblock on my path. It was a possibility—the Show-Cause hearing wasn't an absolute guarantee for people with criminal records. But in the back of my mind, I think I knew.

A couple of weeks later, the letter I'd been dreading arrived in the mail. I would not be allowed to participate in the swearing-in ceremony with everyone else who had passed the bar the same time I did.

"Ms. Haynes, please be advised that you successfully completed the July 24/25, 2012 Tennessee bar examination," it read. "However, you are not eligible to receive a Tennessee law license pending Board approval of your application. You will be notified by the Board of Law Examiners if you must appear before the Board and provide supplemental information regarding any part of your application."

A couple of weeks after that, they officially gave me the news. I was informed that there would be a Show-Cause hearing to determine my admittance—scheduled for December of that year.

———

NEITHER PETER NOR I HAD A CLUE ABOUT WHAT TO EXPECT OR HOW TO prepare. He had never handled a Show-Cause hearing before, and the letter itself didn't reveal much. It came with no guidelines or structure beyond the instructions to show up at the Tennessee Board of Law Examiners' office at a certain time. And so, operating totally in the dark, we set out to make up our own rules.

After reaching out to a few people in Peter's network for advice, we decided to pull from techniques we'd used at my trials in the past. To make a case for myself in my own words, we would use the format of a direct-examination, with Peter asking me detailed questions about all the strides I'd made since leaving prison. Through our back-and-forths, we would work together as a team to build a picture of who I was now.

Peter thought it would also be a good idea to have people at the hearing vouch for my character. Like the packet we pulled together for my resentencing hearing—filled with testimonies about me from friends and family and the women at Alderson—we would call on the people from my community who supported me most. I reached out to Dean Townzen at NSL, who had anticipated what the Tennessee Board of Law Examiners might need to be convinced that I was fit to practice and was invested in giving me tools for my success from the very beginning.

I also reached out to Joe Ravenell at Mount Zion's prison ministry. Mr. Ravenell had been open to my ideas. He had listened to me—centering my voice and experiences—and because of his faith in my vision, I was able to realize my desire to do something around reentry work within the church. As it happened, he was also an investigator at the federal Public Defender's Office and formerly in the secret service. Having him there, given his background and experience, would be huge. Dawn Deaner from the Public Defender's Office also agreed to speak, along with two of Peter's colleagues at his law firm—a partner and a former judge. Each one of these people, in their own way, embodied the second-chance culture that had made so many of my achievements up to this point possible.

On the day of the hearing, Peter and I walked down to the Board of Law Examiners' office together—it was just a short walk from our office—and met the rest of the character witnesses there. After we all arrived, one of the board members finally came out to the lobby to tell us it was our turn. But before anyone could even enter the room to begin, they stopped us. "We know these people," the board member said, gesturing toward the people who'd gathered that day on my behalf. "They're all respected folks in the legal profession—and we know they're all going to come in here and say great things about you, Ms. Haynes." Then, he turned his attention to me: "But we don't want to hear from them. We want to hear directly from you."

Peter and I were prepared to talk *after* everybody else did—that was the plan: each person would come in and talk for two to three minutes, and then Peter and I would follow it up to close. But now, with this sudden shift to the format, we were forced to change course. The five or six faces on the board panel would be looking at me expectantly. *We want to hear directly from you.*

And so, like we'd done so many times in the past, Peter and I walked into the room alone, suiting up for battle. He became my lawyer once again, and together, we told my story. We walked through the main points in my case—meeting C, the conviction, the appeals won and lost. But mostly, we talked about my life after Alderson—what they needed to know to really understand who I was now. We talked about the dream I'd had to go to law school since college, and my commitment to seeing it through, no matter how drastically my circumstances had changed.

Peter asked me about the prison ministry at Mount Zion, where my passions around improving the reentry process for other formerly incarcerated people deepened. I detailed all the work I'd done for my community—going back into the halfway house where I was once a resident and into so many others to provide useful resources for residents, designed entirely around what they expressed their needs to be. We also talked about the future. That I wanted to become a public defender so that I could impact the system in a meaningful way, however I could.

When Peter and I finished, the members of the panel looked at each other. Not a single one of them had any follow-up questions. "Well," they said finally, "usually we send out a letter with our decision, but we're going to let you know right now."

"We're granting you your law license, Ms. Haynes." It was at this point that I took the time to really look at each of the faces in the room, and I saw that they were all smiling at me. Every one of them said that they were proud of me and of the work I was doing.

After all the hoops, all the hurdles, all the barriers to getting here, it all came down to this. I exhaled, saying a silent prayer of gratitude.

———

ON DECEMBER 12, 2012—ALMOST SIX YEARS TO THE DAY SINCE I'D boarded that little plane in Beckley, leaving behind Alderson for good—I was sworn in, officially, as an attorney in the state of Tennessee. We held the ceremony at Peter's office, with Judge Cantrell—the retired judge who worked with us at the law firm—presiding. The event was small and intimate. Surrounded by my family and friends and coworkers, inside a place that had come to mean so much to me over the years, I held up my right hand as Judge Cantrell led me through the attorney's oath:

"I, Keeda Haynes," I repeated, "do solemnly swear or affirm that I will support the Constitution of the United States and the Constitution of the State of Tennessee. In the practice of my profession, I will conduct myself with honesty, fairness, integrity, and civility to the best of my skill and abilities, so help me God."

Standing in the window, looking out over the skyline of downtown Nashville—a Christmas tree reflected in the window—I thought about the women at Alderson. They had believed in me and my innocence and had encouraged me when I needed it the most. As much as this moment, this accomplishment, was for me, it was also for them and for the so many others I had yet to meet. They were still right there with me, in my pocket. And I was going to continue to take them wherever I would go next.

I smiled and wiped a tear thinking of them, knowing they would be proud. Then, I turned back to the small crowd that had gathered: My family and friends, who had been there supporting me all along the way. Peter, who had fought for me tirelessly throughout this entire process—even if he couldn't get rid of my conviction, he was constantly helping me fulfill my dream.

Tonight, I thought, *we celebrate.* Tomorrow, the work begins.

chapter 22

A FEW MONTHS AFTER MY SWEARING-IN CEREMONY, I GOT A CALL from the Public Defender's Office to come in for an interview. By that June of 2013, I was packing up my things at Peter's law firm to begin my new position as assistant public defender for Metropolitan Nashville–Davidson County.

This was my opportunity—the moment I had long been working for. Finally, I would have the chance to ensure that those moving through the system were not subjected to the same mistreatment I was. Finally, I could begin the work I set out to do eight years before when I announced my intentions in front of Judge Trauger at my resentencing hearing:

If I can prevent one person from having to walk down this road that I have been down, I had said, *then it would all be worth it.*

Of all the people in my world whose belief and support helped me get to this important milestone, in the weeks before my start at the Public Defender's Office I found myself thinking about my grandmother Pinky the most. Pinky, who had always made all of her grandchildren feel uniquely special and loved. Who showed up for us, always, whenever we needed anything. Pinky, who was there for each crazy turn in my life over these last few years, offering her words, her faith, and her encouragement. She was a reassuring face during my trial and on the few times I was able to see my family while locked away at Alderson. She was there, among the group of loved ones who welcomed me home at the airport after my release; she cheered for me when I graduated from law school and stood proudly by when I was finally sworn in as an attorney. When I was getting adjusted to my new life in Nashville after leaving prison, Pinky was the only family member who lived close by while everyone else was further away in Franklin. It was Pinky who had driven my car from Franklin when I was allowed to bring it to the halfway house, and who later offered to cosign on my first apartment, wanting to do whatever she could to help me secure it. And it was Pinky, all those years ago, who had kissed my forehead after that intense week of my initial trial and told me that everything was going be all right. Not because these were comforting words to say, but because it was something she truly believed.

Pinky's presence in my life was enormous, and I couldn't believe that she was no longer here.

In March 2013, just three months after my grandmother had watched me recite the attorney's oath in Peter's office, she went into her room to lie down after work, complaining to my sister of a little indigestion, and never woke up again. She died in her sleep.

One minute she was in the world, at the center of my universe, as she'd always been. And the next, she was just . . . gone.

Just as it had been with Sue Lee, before Pinky passed, I had never even thought about what life would be like without her. It was true that Sue Lee was in her eighties and had been sick off and on. But Pinky was seventy-four and didn't look even close to her age. She was healthy and active, her vibrant self, right until the end. The day she died, she'd gone to have lunch with my younger cousins at their school. And when she'd come home from work later, her neighbors remembered having a completely normal conversation with her as they often did, before she went inside. They—like the rest of us who loved her so much—were stunned. "We literally just saw Ms. Pinky driving down the road three hours ago," people who knew her would say, recalling that day.

In the days after, as we all struggled to come to terms with her death, I remember my sister saying that, ultimately, Pinky had died when all of her grandkids were in a good place. Anitra was in a good place with her nursing career. My brothers were in a good place in their lives with jobs and school. And I had just been admitted as an attorney. Finally. Perhaps, the woman who had cared for us so fiercely knew that she had successfully helped us get to where we needed to be.

And it was true. Pinky's passing felt like the close of one chapter and the start of a new one. As I readied myself to embark on this next phase of my journey, I hoped she was looking down on me.

I hoped that I could make her proud.

———

"I AM MY CLIENT, AND MY CLIENT IS ME."

That is what I said when it was my turn to speak. I was sitting in a circle in Birmingham, Alabama, with public defenders from cities across the South, almost forty of us altogether. We were asked why we had chosen to become public defenders.

I was attending a training called Gideon's Promise, on a work assignment with one of my new coworkers shortly after starting my job during the summer of 2013. We were there to learn the essence of "how to fight" for our clients. Over the next two weeks, we would learn skills designed to prepare us as public defenders to effectively advocate for the people we represented. Gideon's Promise, an organization founded by criminal defense attorney Jonathan Rapping, emerged onto the legal landscape in 2007 with a mission to "transform the criminal justice system by building a movement of public defenders who provide equal justice for marginalized communities." Initially concentrated in cities across the South, Gideon's Promise believed in a client-centered approach to public defense work—prioritizing the experiences of marginalized clients, learning their stories, in an effort to provide more holistic and more just representation. Within the legal world, Gideon's was thought of as the gold standard.

Sitting there in the room at the training, I listened to person after person step into the center of the circle and discuss why they had chosen to become a public defender. As I listened, I wondered what I would say.

Of course I knew why I had become a public defender, but in saying so, I would have to acknowledge to a room full of strangers that I had a criminal record. I didn't know these people, and I wasn't up for their judgment. As the number of people left to speak dwindled, my mind began to spin. *How should I answer?* I asked myself. I didn't fully know yet that even sharing my story was a challenge to the systems of privilege and oppression that dictated our lives and work. But I knew in my gut that speaking the truth would create an imbalance in the room.

As each person in the circle stood, spoke, and sat back down, I thought again about everything that I had overcome to be in this moment. I thought about my future clients, about the women back at Alderson, and about the words I'd spoken before Judge Trauger at my resentencing hearing. Then, the thoughts began to form.

But knowing what to say didn't make voicing it any easier—my introvert tendencies pushed the sentences back down into my throat. I never could do large crowds very well.

As the session wore on, I continued to replay the words I *wanted* to say in my head over and over. If I was going to do this—and I knew that I had to—I wanted to make sure that I covered all the necessary bases without getting into too many details.

The room quieted down after another person finished sharing, and the administrators asked for the next volunteer. There were only a few of us left to go. The pressure was building. I glanced around the circle and tentatively stepped forward, feeling forty pairs of eyes staring at me as I did. Then, I took a deep breath and I spoke:

"I am my client, and my client is me."

You could literally hear a pin drop when I said those words. I continued on with the story about being convicted for a crime I didn't commit, serving time in federal prison, and now becoming a public defender. "I want to make sure other people never have to experience what I went through in the system," I told them, saying out loud the same thought I'd repeated in my head so many times.

The next two weeks of training at Gideon's was intense. As a group, we learned and we grew, examining how we could support and advocate for our clients at every stage from the moment they were arrested through each step that came after. We were challenged and we challenged one another on issue after issue. But as the training wore on, I realized that never, in our entire two weeks together, did we have a real conversation about race or systemic racism, and how those factors critically impacted our clients. This would change—both within Gideon's and across the entire legal system—in later years, as the Black Lives Matter movement gained more momentum. But that summer, I don't remember racism ever being named. Even an organization that was doing so much genuine good had its blind spots.

Instead, I noticed how they talked about the blanket "power structure" that put our clients, and ourselves as defenders, at a disadvantage in the criminal legal system. Yes, it was true that we were at a disadvantage; however, I knew from my own experiences, and by hearing the stories of so many others, that the disadvantage was more than a corrupt cop or prosecutor or judge. That it was more than even the limits of the law itself. The entire criminal legal system was built on a foundation of systemic racism. As a Black woman in the South— especially since my arrest—I had lived and seen firsthand just how much the system depended on that foundation. Depended on it to uphold white supremacy, to uphold the imbalances that worked in favor of those who held the power.

In the years to come, I would see even more clearly how much the system depended on that foundation never being named, and the many ways even well-intentioned people carefully avoided naming it.

———

FOR MY FIRST SIX MONTHS ON THE JOB AS A PUBLIC DEFENDER, I WOULD be working in General Sessions—the misdemeanors court. People who came through those doors had been charged with minor offenses—things like trespassing, public intoxication, driving under the influence, domestic violence, drug offenses, and various other misdemeanors that carried no more than eleven months and twenty-nine days in jail. The plan was for me to shadow a few more experienced attorneys for a couple of weeks in the courtrooms to learn the ropes, then after that, I'd begin handling cases on my own.

Going to the courthouse on the first day, I remember the elevator doors opening onto the General Sessions floor and entering into a world of activity. There was movement everywhere: people coming in and out of courtrooms; attorneys huddled with clients, talking through their cases; clients conversating with their families, waiting for their turn to go in; prosecutors arguing with defense attorneys, trying to hammer out plea negotiations. People on their phones—standing, sitting, navigating through all the noise. It was loud and chaotic, and from Day One, I had no choice but to fully dive in.

Almost every day during those first six months working in General Sessions, I sat holed up in my office until late at night, trying to stay on top of the next day's caseload. Even with little downtime during the workday because of the demands of court, I was committed to doing whatever I could, however I could, to get prepared.

The misdemeanors court was constant movement: always on your feet, always in and out of courtrooms. Week after week, I began to see the same faces, the same minor crimes—with poverty often being the common denominator. Trespassing, blocking an entranceway vandalism, just to name a few—these were some of the charges constantly doled out.

As a result, homeless people were forced out of public spaces and arrested for falling asleep on the street or for blocking a sidewalk. Or for taking shelter from the elements—the cold, the rain—in a space where they didn't "belong." I remember one case I had where my client was arrested for trespassing. It was pouring raining, and he was standing under the awning of a church, trying not to get drenched. Apparently, he and a few other people he was with had been warned before about not going near this church. But it was wet and miserable out, and they had nowhere else to go. And they were criminally penalized for it.

Time and time again, cases like these came across my desk. People charged or locked up for nothing more than the unfortunate circumstances of their lives.

The longer I spent in General Sessions, the more aware I became of this fact. People with untreated mental health issues, arrested for things like disorderly conduct. People struggling with addiction, arrested for having drug paraphernalia or a small amount of drugs for personal use. And those most likely to be arrested for these things? Almost always—*always*—Black, brown, and poor people. The system made its priorities clear: It was criminalizing homelessness. It was criminalizing mental health. It was criminalizing addiction. It was ultimately criminalizing poverty. And, of course, it was criminalizing race. The truth of this was evident in the jail dockets I worked through day after day.

It was the complete disregard of the whole person—and all the complex, overlapping issues they came with—that fueled the criminal legal system as it was.

At the end of the day, I realized that people were just being processed through—one after the next, after the next—and all I could try to do was stem the tide. Every day in the office, I had my eyes opened wider and wider to all the ways in which this was devastatingly true. We were taught early on that our job was to "put out the fires," and we had become really good at it. Client after client after client—putting out fire, after fire, after fire. But what I realized was that no one was asking *who* was starting the fires and *why*.

When I first applied to the Public Defender's Office, my vision for the role was a corrective one: the system had failed me, and I took the job thinking I could help stop that from happening to others. But over time, what I was slowly learning was that the system hadn't actually failed me—because it was never designed for my success in the first place. The existing criminal justice system did to me exactly what it is made to do. It did the same thing to me that it does to countless other people: stacking the weight of systemic racism against someone who has no hope of beating it, then extracting whatever it can.

During those initial months in General Sessions, this fact became crystal clear.

———

CHAPTER 22

AFTER WORKING IN GENERAL SESSIONS FOR SEVERAL MONTHS, I WAS moved to Criminal Court. There, I was assigned to the courtroom of an elderly white man who had been on the bench for years. He wasn't known to be the best judge in criminal court, but he wasn't the worst one either—many thought that title belonged to two other Criminal Court judges, depending on the color of your skin, how much money you had, and who you asked. I had heard horror stories about the extensive time these judges gave young Black men in their courtrooms, and how the district attorneys—or DAs—assigned to those courtrooms were just as terrible as the judges. I had no desire to practice in either of those courtrooms, so I was glad that I wasn't assigned to them.

I was excited about this move to Criminal Court, not because I was looking forward to having to practice in front of yet *another* older white judge, but because General Sessions had been a complete zoo. Working there, I never felt as if I had the time to fully prepare for my cases. When working the jail docket, we often wouldn't find out who our clients were until the day before the court date, which prevented us from effectively preparing for our cases in court. Even when we had cases on the bond dockets, because of the volume of cases that we had to handle, there was never enough time to prepare for those cases either.

Working in Criminal Court would be different. While we still had a heavy caseload, there was at least a little more time to prepare. Having more time to think and research, without having to do so much of the work on our feet, spur-of-the-moment, worked much better for me. I was the person who always liked to review all of the discovery in a case several times and to take notes. I loved research-ing the potential issues in the cases and being active in the inves-tigations with the investigators. (I'm sure the investigators didn't like it so much, but I wanted to be involved in every aspect of my clients' cases.) In General Sessions, doing these things was nearly impossible.

While I had more time to prep for my cases than I did in General Sessions, Criminal Court came with its own set of issues. In Criminal Court, the stakes for my clients were higher. There, my clients were facing anywhere from one year to possible life in prison. Thankfully, in my years in the Public Defender's Office, I never had a case where a client was given life, but even so, because of the time that my clients *were* facing, it made the injustices—from vengeful DAs to lying police officers and biased judges—that much more egregious. Not all of the DAs were vengeful; not all of the police lied (though many did); not all of the judges I encountered were biased. But all it takes is *one* of these factors to negatively impact your client, sometimes for the rest of their lives. Imagine the level of impact for a client if they're faced with a combination of the above factors. And most of the time, they were. Like in the case of Chris Rice.

Chris was a fifty-plus-year-old Black man. (I called my clients by their first names, and I asked that they do the same for me. I felt strongly that adopting this practice removed some of the power dynamics often in place between attorneys and clients. I wanted my clients to be comfortable with me.) Like most poor Black men in the community, those who had been victims of the War on Drugs in the 1980s, 1990s, and 2000s, Chris had a few felony drug charges on his record as well as some petty misdemeanor drug and trespassing charges. Because his criminal record prevented him from securing stable housing and employment, he was transient, living between his mother's and his brother's homes in public housing. At the time of the incident he was arrested for, Chris was staying with his brother in a very small one-bedroom public housing apartment.

CHAPTER 22

The judge appointed me to Chris's case after he was indicted in Criminal Court. He was charged with being a felon in possession of a firearm, and with various felony drug charges.

All of these charges stemmed from a search warrant into Chris's brother's home where Chris was currently living. When I arraigned the case in court, we entered a plea of not guilty.

As was customary, I filed a motion for discovery so that the state could turn over the evidence they had regarding Chris's case. In the discovery was a search warrant, which established the probable cause the police relied on to be granted access to search Chris's home. When I initially read the search warrant, I couldn't believe that the officers had said the warrant was based on seeing the end of a marijuana joint in Chris's trash can in his living room. The police said that Chris granted them permission to enter the home after a "knock and talk"—a police technique that involves knocking on the front door of a private residence and asking for consent before entering. But when I met with Chris to discuss the case, he completely denied he had given the officers permission to come into his home.

He told me that he was asleep when the police came. "They were banging really hard on the front and back doors at the same time," he explained in my office one afternoon. The banging on the front door eventually stopped, he'd said, but they kept on knocking forcefully at the back door. Chris got up and went to the rear of the apartment. When he opened the back door, he found one of the police officers standing on the back porch, who instructed Chris to open the front door for the rest of the officers who were still there, knocking away. Chris headed to the opposite end of the apartment, and when he opened the front door, he found two more officers standing there and a third positioned on the side of the yard. As Chris talked to them, the officer standing at the back door walked into the house.

Of course, the officer would report later that Chris had given him permission to enter, but Chris was adamant that he had not.

Chris said that as the officer at the back of the apartment walked through the house, he bent down and looked inside a small trash can beside the couch, where the officer says he saw what he thought was the end of a joint. Chris said that there was nothing in the trash can because he had just emptied it. On the basis of what they "alleged" they had seen in that trash can, the police froze the scene and were granted a warrant to search Chris's home.

As Chris and I continued to go through the details of his case that afternoon, he told me that he strongly believed that the officers were lying and that they had violated his rights. I agreed with him and immediately began the research process to support this issue. We would file a motion to suppress, arguing that Chris's Fourth Amendment right to protection against unreasonable searches and seizures had been violated. Therefore, any evidence against him the police had obtained during their illegal search should be marked as inadmissible in court. This is what the motion to suppress would allow us to do.

Not only was this issue important to Chris, but it was important to me as well. This was not the first time that I had handled a case in which the police officer had lied and violated my client's constitutional rights. The first instance involved Hector Gonzalez, an undocumented client I once represented, who was arrested and taken to jail after a traffic stop, under the claim that his tags had expired. Fortunately, Hector was able to make bond before Immigration and Customs Enforcement (ICE) put a hold on him to deport him.

Prior to Hector's court date, I contacted the Department of Transportation and the dealership where Hector had purchased his car— both confirmed that Hector's tags had not expired on the day he was stopped and arrested. They sent over the documentation to verify all of this, and when I passed it on to the district attorney in charge of handling the case, they ultimately agreed to dismiss the charges.

It was clear that the police had lied and that racial profiling was more than likely involved. Hector and I were both furious that the arresting officer had made up an excuse in his citation, and Hector asked me what, if anything, could be done. I told him that with his permission I could file a complaint against the officer with the Nashville Police Department's Office of Professional Accountability (OPA). He agreed and I filed the complaint, along with the documentation we'd collected to support it. I spoke to the sergeant assigned to investigate the complaint, reiterating that the arresting officer had lied and attributing the source of his lie to his own implicit biases. After reviewing the information, the sergeant called me back and told me that the officer was neither racist nor biased against Hispanic individuals because his niece was Hispanic, and that everyone had also said that he is the nicest officer and is very nice to everyone.

The sergeant told me that, in spite of the documentation I had submitted, he was going to put in the officer's file that the complaint was "unfounded," and recommend that the officer take additional classes on writing citations. Needless to say, Hector and I were both angry. My client could easily have been deported because of the officer's harmful actions—his lies—and it was apparent that the OPA would do nothing to rectify it. It was clear whose side they were on. During my time in the Public Defender's Office, I filed several other complaints against officers for lying in arrest warrants and search warrants, and every single time OPA concluded the complaints were unfounded.

And the police wonder why the public feels such distrust toward them.

On the day of Chris's hearing, the state put all of the officers involved on the stand to testify. Two of the officers said they didn't hear anything, but the other two—those Chris directly spoke with at the front and the back of the apartment—stated, under oath, that Chris had expressly given them permission to enter. "Please open the front door for the other officers," the cop Chris had spoken to at the back door said he told Chris—and Chris allegedly complied. Hearing this, I didn't know whether to laugh or scream! In my experience, flex officers—those specifically assigned to "ferret out" neighborhood crime, who also regularly violate people's rights in the process—never ask the Black men they encounter in public housing to *"please"* do anything.

After my cross-examination—during which the officers continued to insist that Chris had given permission to enter his home—Chris himself prepared to take the stand. Normally, clients don't testify at suppression hearings, but Chris wanted to. "I'm not lying, and I want to testify," he told me in the days before, as we were getting ready for the hearing. I knew what it felt like to want to defend yourself, in your own words, against attacks on your character. To be committed to telling the facts, the truth—even if it's clear that those in the room holding the power may not be open to hearing it. And so, we worked together to prepare Chris to take the stand.

I knew that the state would bring up Chris's prior criminal record to discredit him, and, of course, that's exactly what they did. But Chris held his own. He admitted to his record but was very firm in his responses that he had not given the officers permission to enter his home. The detailed account he gave in the courtroom that day was exactly the same as the one he'd recounted to me when we first met.

At the close of proof, I made my arguments that the officers had violated Chris's Fourth Amendment constitutional right to be protected from unreasonable searches and seizures. "Ms. Haynes, are you saying that the officers violated Mr. Rice's constitutional rights by going around to the back of his house to seek entrance?" the judge interrupted in the middle of one of my arguments. "Yes, Judge," I responded, a little surprised by his interjection. I went on to explain how private homeowners have a reasonable expectation of privacy, and that neither he nor I would expect to see a police officer knocking on our back doors out of the blue. "But Ms. Haynes, Mr. Rice lives in public housing," he responded, as if to justify the violation.

I had been prepared to make additional arguments about why the officers had violated Chris's constitutional rights, but when I heard the judge make this statement, I was stunned. I actually had to take a few moments to gather myself up before I could continue. "Judge," I responded, after taking a breath. "Are you telling me that you believe that just because someone lives in public housing that they do not have the same constitutional rights as you and me?" Seconds passed between us in silence, as the judge just looked at me. But there was no mistaking what this elderly, white man who would make this decision really thought.

Fuming but undeterred, I pressed on with my arguments. While discussing that Chris had adamantly denied giving the officers permission to enter his home, pointing out the differences in the officers' versions of "permission," the judge interrupted me once again:

"Ms. Haynes, do you expect me to take the word of a ten-time felon over these officers?"

I replied as calmly as I could manage. "Yes Judge, I do. And here's why." I continued with my argument in support of my client, point by point. In the end, the judge said that he would take the matter under advisement and issue a written order.

After the hearing, I was livid, but Chris's attitude was even, his emotions under control. "Ms. Keeda, listen: you did great. We did all we could do," he told me in his ever so calm voice. "I'm not mad. I'm used to the police lying, and people not believing me—I am a Black man and a felon . . . It's okay."

But it wasn't okay, not for me it wasn't. It broke my heart that Chris had grown accustomed to being treated like this by the criminal legal system, by white people, and by police officers—to the point where he had just accepted it as a way of life. But this was the reality. And not just for Chris, but for many of my clients. So many times, I would hear them say that a police officer was lying about what had happened in their case, and that a judge would never believe them over the police because they were Black and/or had a record. But that didn't stop me from fighting. It never did. To the contrary, it pushed me to fight harder.

When the judge on Chris's case finally issued his ruling, as expected, he denied our motion to suppress. He restated some of the reasons he had given in court on the day of the hearing. We immediately filed the necessary paperwork to start the appellate process. The judge was wrong, and as long as Chris was willing to fight, so was I. I kept Chris out on bond as long as I could before he had to enter a plea to one of the felony drug charges and was sentenced to three years in prison.

Throughout his sentence, Chris would write to let me know that he was doing okay, and we would talk about his appeal. Another attorney in the office was handling it, but I tried to stay involved as much as I could. When I eventually heard that Chris's appeal was denied, I went to see him. On the day I visited, he reassured me that he was fine and that he wasn't expecting to win anyway. "Thank you for fighting for me," he told me. "I've been in and out of the system for a while, and in all of those times, I've never had a public defender fight for me like you did." Chris said he had almost finished his three-year sentence and was scheduled to be released soon.

CHAPTER 22

I have run into Chris in the community a few times since his release. Every time I see him, he still calls me "Ms. Keeda." We hug and talk about what he's doing now. He tells me about his latest job and where he is living. He tells me that he's doing well. And as we part ways, he smiles and tells whomever he is with, "That's my lawyer."

———

I CONTINUED WORKING IN CHRIS'S JUDGE'S COURTROOM, HANDLING the cases that were assigned to me. But I admit it was hard. With every interaction this judge had with my clients, I thought about the remarks he made during that hearing. I lost all respect for him after what he said about Chris Rice—words that were not just about Chris but about every poor person who lived in public housing because of the lack of affordable housing in Nashville or because they were unemployed or underemployed. Being poor should never mean you must forfeit your constitutional rights. But, unfortunately, this judge's thinking about my Black, brown, and poor clients was not unique to him. It was the same way the district attorneys thought of them. It was the same way that many police officers thought and other judges too. It's the way society thinks as a whole.

Experiences like these continued to cement my understanding of what most of my clients already knew: there truly is no justice in the criminal justice system.

As the years passed in the Public Defender's Office, my realizations about how terrible the criminal "justice" system truly was only deepened. And so did my commitment to speak openly about it.

Then, during the summer of 2016, three years into my job, my colleague Sarah walked into my office as I sat at my desk, preparing for the next day in court.

Sarah was the communications director at the office. She had essentially taken on the role of diversity coordinator as well. In my unrelenting efforts to center the issue of race in discussions of culture at the office and of the criminal system, Sarah and I often ended up talking in each other's offices.

"I told a reporter at the *Nashville Scene* about your story and suggested he write an article about you," she said to me that day.

She saw the reluctance on my face right away—I was comfortable telling my own story, but I was a lot less comfortable with someone else telling it.

"Steven's a friendly reporter," she reassured me. "Trust me, he understands what's going on." I finally agreed, and she said that she would have Steven give me a call.

A couple of weeks later, when Steven came to my office, I was still hesitant. During our interview, I remember the way he took notes without looking at his notepad as we talked. The conversation didn't last any longer than an hour, and then we were done.

Steven left my office and I continued with my work. A few weeks later, a photographer from the *Scene* contacted me to set up a time to take some photos for the article.

I had court that day, so they wanted to come with me to take pictures in the courtroom. I was on the misdemeanor review docket. The few clients I had on my docket that day would be pleading guilty to time served on BS charges.

I turned in my pleas to the clerk and was waiting for my clients to be brought in from the back lockup. As I waited, Mr. Johnson walked into the courtroom. He had been late for court. The room was relatively empty: All of the other attorneys were gone except for me and the police officers who had been subpoenaed for court. The judge asked me if the Public Defender's Office could represent Mr. Johnson. I did a quick conflict check and determined that there wasn't one, and the judge appointed me to represent Mr. Johnson. You never want to represent a client you just met that same day at a preliminary hearing, but what other choice did we have?

I talked with Mr. Johnson about his case—a felony drug charge—going through the warrant line by line. Not surprisingly, the incident Mr. Johnson described to me was completely different from what the officers alleged to have happened in the warrant. The arresting officers were part of the Nashville Police Department's Crime Suppression Unit (CSU), a group that was well-known to overpolice Black neighborhoods and harass Black people. I had argued a lot of Fourth

Amendment violation cases (unreasonable search and seizures) that started with this unit, and I knew the applicable case law that I would use from memory.

Cases are hardly ever dismissed at preliminary hearings, but if there was a judge that would dismiss them, this judge was the one. It was obvious from the start that the officer was not telling the truth on the stand, and that Mr. Johnson had legitimate Fourth Amendment issues. The judge said that it was a close call, but bound the case over to the Grand Jury. It wasn't an outright dismissal, but we had set the case up for a very good motion to suppress in Criminal Court.

I had gotten so caught up in the hearing that I had forgotten the photographer from the *Scene* was in the room taking pictures. He had truly captured me in my element, arguing for my client with my full attention and energy.

Always, in those moments, nothing mattered more than the people I represented.

———

THE MORNING THE ARTICLE WAS RELEASED, I HAD FORGOTTEN THAT IT was coming out. It wasn't until a few hours after it was published that I remembered.

I nearly dropped my phone when I read the first line.

Steven had asked me what my first thought was when I got to the compound at Alderson. I remember telling him that I was looking around in disbelief thinking, "I'm in fucking federal prison."

And those were the words staring back at me from the opening lines of the story. I started thinking about my dad, the minister, reading it. I thought of my own pastor reading it as well. I couldn't even read the rest of the article because I was stuck on those five words.

But that didn't stop anyone else from reading. By the time I had gotten to court that morning, all of my colleagues had read it. The prosecutors, judges, probation officers, and all of my family and friends. It was being shared all over social media.

I assumed that most people at the courthouse knew about my background before the article came out, but apparently not. I am not a person who likes to be in the spotlight, so all of the attention was very overwhelming for me. The judge whose courtroom I was assigned to at that time called me back into his office after docket call to tell me that he had read the story and that he was proud of me and all that I had accomplished. "Now, I can really see where your tenacity to fight for your clients comes from," he told me.

Most of my clients knew about my background or learned of it very quickly upon my representation because, well, people talk. I was always very forthcoming with them about it when they asked. Having a felony on my record gave me a form of "street cred" with them. Some asked questions about the specifics of the case, my co-defendants, and even my prison experience. Most wanted to know how I was able to become a lawyer with a felony on my record. They seemed almost in awe of this accomplishment and wanted to know how I did it. Some even expressed interest in getting degrees themselves when released. But for my clients and others who were incarcerated who did not know, they definitely found out after the *Nashville Scene* article was published.

In the weeks and months after the piece was released, I received an incredible number of letters from men and women incarcerated in state and federal prisons across the country. Somehow or other they had read the article or seen it republished on other websites and felt they had to reach out. Some people asked for help with their cases. They felt that if anyone could understand the injustices they were experiencing, it would be someone like me, who had endured the same kinds of injustices personally. It was heartbreaking to read the various things that people were going through at the hands of the criminal legal system. While some asked for help, most just wanted someone to listen, and to feel heard. Others wrote simply to congratulate me on my success; they felt that I had beaten the odds, and my story gave them hope that they could too.

I remember one afternoon, going to retrieve my mail from the office mailbox, as I did most days after court. Picking up my stack of letters, I flipped through several pertaining to bar membership, a few pieces of correspondence from clients, and miscellaneous junk mail. And then, an envelope stamped with bold black letters reading "Legal Mail" caught my eye. I didn't recognize the sender's name—Stephanie Lane—but the return address was immediately familiar. "Alderson Federal Prison Camp," the place I spent nearly four years of my life, was printed neatly on the top left corner.

I opened the letter and began reading. Stephanie introduced herself, telling me that she was serving time on a federal drug charge at Alderson. She acknowledged that she and I had never met but that she had heard about me and my story and wanted to write me. She told me that one of the few—if not the only—Black male officers at Alderson during the time I was there was now a case manager and had brought my *Nashville Scene* article into the facility for the women to read. Stephanie described how the article had been copied and passed around the entire compound. In ending her letter, she told me that all of the women were proud of me and that I was an inspiration to them all. She wished me well and said that they were all rooting for me.

The letters from people who were incarcerated continued to come, along with the outpouring of emails from people across the country. I also continued to speak on panels and started accepting invitations to be part of committees regarding criminal justice reform—on top of my duties representing my clients in court.

Even after the wave of messages slowed down after the initial release of the article, I still received them from time to time. I appreciated each and every one, but those coming from women in federal prison were always special to me. The bond I felt with them was especially strong. I knew so much of what these women were going through. There was a certain kinship, the feeling of belonging to the same club—as if we were all sisters, bound together by the injustices of the federal legal system. While I didn't know the women personally, it was as if my success was their success. And as much as they may have been inspired by my story, they were as much an inspiration for me in all the work I was pushing to do.

There was another letter I received that particularly stands out for me. It was from a young lady named Ashley Starling, who was in federal prison in Bryan, Texas. She wrote to tell me how much of an inspiration I had been to her and the women at Bryan. Our cases and backgrounds were very similar, and she said that her federal public defender had sent her my article after her own devasting loss at trial. My story, Starling explained, had given her hope when she felt that there was nothing left to hope for. After reading about me, she had a different perspective about her situation and what she was currently going through.

Starling also shared that she was a writer and had written an article in the camp's newsletter for Black History Month. She included a copy of the newsletter along with her note, and reading through it, I was reminded how creative incarcerated people are. The theme of the edition was titled "Ordinary People Change the World." A quote by Maya Angelou opened the issue, followed by a paragraph describing the story of Black History Month. Inside, Starling decided to write about me and my experience with the criminal justice system, and how I had overcome so many obstacles. Out of all of the courageous, heroic Black women, past and present, who have inspired so many with their work and their lives, I couldn't believe that she had decided to write about me. "Keeda's life demonstrates that past mistakes do not determine your future," she wrote. "Coming to prison doesn't have to be a roadblock. We can turn it into a stepping-stone, and Keeda Haynes is living proof that it's possible."

As I read those words, tears began to well up in my eyes. I finished the rest of the newsletter and placed it back inside the envelope with Starling's note. I opened my desk drawer and put it with all of the other letters from incarcerated people that I had been receiving.

It was in this moment, reading Starling's letter, that I finally let myself really and truly examine my life and all the obstacles I had overcome to get to here. For so much of my journey, I had been so fixated on ensuring that no one else experienced the things I had in the legal system, on dismantling this system built on systemic racism and upheld by white supremacy, that I hadn't really stopped to take it all in.

It was true that there weren't a lot of formerly incarcerated people who had accomplished the things that I had, and yes, I would always fight for reentry reform. But I realized that fighting for others to have the same opportunities that I had doesn't diminish what I was able to accomplish. It definitely had not been an easy road. There were some tough fights along the way and many lonely nights. There were times when I was tired and stressed and went to bed thinking how I would make it through another day. But I did. I pressed on, I carried on and confronted every obstacle in my way. Closing my eyes and letting the memories of the pain, hardship, ridicule, joy, strength, and determination wash over me, I realized and embraced the fact that yes, I had beaten the system. I was living proof.

———

AFTER THE ARTICLE WAS PUBLISHED, I STARTED GETTING RECOGNITION from my community—honors and awards—including one from the African American Heritage Society in my hometown, an institution devoted to celebrating the local Black community in Franklin. I also received a wave of invitations to speak publicly about my story—at conferences and universities, Black churches and women's prisons—all across the country.

A few months after the article came out, I was asked to speak at the General Sessions Judge's Conference in Nashville. One of the General Sessions judges from another county had heard about my story and reached out to my boss. When I spoke with the judge, he explained that this was the yearly conference where all of the General Sessions judges from across the state would be convening. He said that after learning my story, he felt strongly that each of the judges in attendance should learn it too.

After hanging up the phone, I thought about what it would mean to be speaking to all of the General Sessions judges from the state of Tennessee, even the ones I practiced in front of daily. I started to realize just how huge this opportunity was—not just for me but, more importantly, for my clients and our communities. This was an opportunity to indict the judges that I practiced in front of on their inhumane treatment of the people who stand before them every single day in court.

This was my chance to say what I couldn't say in their courtrooms, and I was going to seize this moment.

Because of the magnitude of what was at stake with this speech, I wanted to make sure that it was as perfect as it could be. I didn't want to just "tell" my story, I wanted to tell my clients' stories and their realities with the criminal justice system. "I am my client and my client is me" had kind of become the core theme for the speeches that I gave. Generally, those speeches centered around how I am no different than the clients I represent. But this time was different.

As I was sitting at my desk one evening, long after everyone else had left the office for the day (being the last one to leave was not unusual), I began to think about what I would say.

Yes, like my clients, I was dehumanized by the criminal legal system. Yes, like them, I was harassed by the police, and my face was plastered all over the news. Like my clients, I wasn't afforded the presumption of innocence that the Constitution guarantees us, and if I had had a criminal record, I'm sure that would have been used to discredit me as well. Yes, I was locked up, disrespected, and stripped of every ounce of my dignity. My name was no longer my name; instead I became nothing but a number. Yes, I was told when to eat and when to sleep. Yes, I was forced to perform essentially unpaid labor. From the moment I walked through those gates at Alderson, yes, I became a slave. And like almost every single one of my clients, I had experienced my share of collateral consequences upon my release, although the fact that I was sitting in this chair as a public defender, typing up a speech to deliver in front of judges, might indicate to some that I had overcome those collateral consequences.

But that's where the similarities ended. As I continued to reflect on my own situation, coupled with the knowledge that I had gained from my clients and their realities, I started to ask myself: Is my client *really* me?

Unlike my clients, at my initial appearance, I was fortunate to have had a family that could afford to pay for a private attorney on my behalf. Because I was only working a retail job at the time, I'm sure that I would have qualified for a federal public defender. I would like to think that my judge would not have violated my Sixth Amendment right to representation. I would hope that I wouldn't be forced to go up against the power of the government without a well-trained attorney or threatened to be locked up for asking for an attorney, like a few of the judges in the courthouse would often do to my clients. Being poor is a hardship, not a crime, and should never be treated as such.

Unlike most of my clients, after my initial arrest I was released on my own recognizance and was only able to maintain my innocence and exercise my right to a trial because I wasn't in custody. This afforded me the opportunity to work with my attorney on the case; it allowed for it to be investigated and for all necessary motions to be filed on my behalf. It also allowed me to continue to work, and, even more importantly, it gave me the opportunity to finish my undergraduate degree in criminal justice and psychology.

According to the Prison Policy Initiative, over five hundred thousand human beings are held in detention facilities across America without being convicted or sentenced. Many are there because they are too poor to make bond. My economically disadvantaged clients who cannot afford their bail are too often stuck in cages before their cases go to trial. Because of this, they are unable to assist in a meaningful way with their cases. Furthermore, being imprisoned in overcrowded jails often translates into clients losing jobs, homes, and sometimes even children. This results in many of my clients pleading guilty to crimes they haven't committed just so they don't have to continue to sit in jail. This money bail system is a wealth-based system that unjustly incarcerates my clients and does nothing to promote public safety. It criminalizes and perpetuates a cycle of poverty and racial inequality in the criminal legal system. My Black and brown clients are held in cages awaiting trial while their white counterparts go free. This is just one example of how America operates two distinct justice systems: one for the wealthy people and one for Black and brown people.

Upon my release, I did have my share of collateral consequences, but I was still able to get a job within days of being back in Nashville. I was able to find housing, received an advanced degree, got my voting rights restored, and had the support of family and friends all along the way. In the eyes of the reentry world, I was the poster child for second chances. But what about my clients who are poor, underemployed, or unemployed? Those with limited education? Clients struggling with unstable housing or homelessness? Those with little or no support from family or friends?

It's hard to have a second chance, when you haven't even been afforded a first chance.

As I continued to think through my speech for the conference, I was reminded of an interview Martin Luther King Jr. gave in May of 1967—eleven months before his assassination. In it, he discusses the "new phase" of the civil rights movement. In response to a question by the interviewer about why the Negro, compared to other minority groups, had such a hard time being successful, King walks through the history of what Black people have experienced since they were first brought to this country as chattel. He describes how after the Emancipation Proclamation was enacted in 1863, we were afforded zero economic foothold to start our new, "free" lives. Around this same time, white Europeans were given land in the West and the North, but Black people received nothing. "Emancipation for the Negro was really freedom to hunger," King said during the interview. "It was freedom without food to eat or land to cultivate, and therefore was freedom and famine at the same time."

King goes on to point out the hypocrisy in white America's message for Black people to pull themselves up by their own bootstraps. Sure, we should all do what we can for ourselves to succeed. But "it is a cruel jest to say to a bootless man that he ought to lift himself up by his own bootstraps," he explains. By overlooking the destructive legacy of slavery and oppression in America, those criticisms ignore the factors responsible for why so many Black people in this country have been left bootless in the first place.

With every new client who walked through my door, I saw over and over how the system was designed to keep Black and brown people bootless—not just the criminal justice system but the entire system surrounding us. An education system that criminalized Black and brown children from kindergarten. A housing system that made it impossible to find a stable home if you'd ever struggled financially or been convicted of a crime. A system that treated opioid addiction as a health care crisis but crack addiction as a crime and a personal failing.

Every day, I witnessed just how much the system was designed not for justice but rather to keep people afraid and impoverished and to trap desperate people in ever-deepening cycles of poverty.

The same way that Martin Luther King Jr. wanted to force the leaders in Washington to see, hear, and *deal* with the problems of racial inequality in this country is the same way that I wanted the judges during this conference to see, hear, and respond to the issues of racial inequality in the criminal justice system.

When the day came to stand in front of those judges, I not only knew the "story" I wanted to tell but the "stories" I *had* to tell.

————

BUT EVEN AS I CONTINUED TO FIGHT TOOTH AND NAIL FOR MY CLIENTS over the years, even as I built relationships and deep trust, it was impossible for me to ignore that by working in the Public Defender's Office, I was, despite it all, part of a system that was designed and determined to keep my clients bootless. And this began to wear on me.

Day after day, I saw my clients being locked up or disrespected by a system that cared nothing about them because they were poor or Black—or both. The realization was especially evident one day when Erika, a young Black client of mine, was late to court, and the judge threatened to put her in the back and lock her up. We tried to explain to the judge that she was late because she had to drop her oldest daughter off at school and had car trouble. But the judge didn't care.

She sent Erika to the back while her three-year-old daughter looked on—wide-eyed and afraid—as her mom was taken away. Erika's daughter started to cry like any kid would. "You need to call someone to come get your child," the judge responded, irritated. But Erika had no one to call. After yelling at her even more for being late, for not having childcare during this appearance, the judge eventually allowed Erika to stay in the courtroom with her daughter.

By the way Erika was treated, you would have thought she was there on a serious felony drug charge. But she wasn't. Erika was in court because she had not paid the fees and fines that had accumulated on a previous case from a few years ago. Because of this, her driver's license had been suspended. Yep, Erika was in court—again—simply because she was poor. The agreement that had been worked out during the previous case was that Erika was to take a driver's license class with the state, then bring proof of completion to court during this appearance, and her case would be dismissed. But Erika still did not have a valid driver's license. The class that Erika had to take cost $75, and Judge Turner wasn't big on waiving that cost for my clients.

Keeping us waiting until the very end of court, the judge called Erika to the podium. We walked to the front of the room together, and I stood beside her, as close as I could, thinking that my proximity could shield her from what was to come. I explained to the judge why Erika hadn't completed the $75 driving course yet: she had recently become homeless, and was now living in her car with her three daughters. She had just gotten hired at McDonald's—a job she was now in jeopardy of losing because she was missing work to be here, in court. And even with this income coming in, the money she was earning wasn't enough to cover all of her and her daughters' expenses, and no one in her family was able to help her financially to fill in the gaps. I took a deep breath, as I had gotten choked up and had to fight back tears at the sheer magnitude of Erika's situation. *What are we doing to people?* I thought to myself, shaking my head in disbelief. Out of the corner of my eye, I saw that Erika had hung her head in shame as I spoke about the circumstances of her life to a courtroom full of people.

As the judge continued to humiliate her, sternly explaining that she had one more chance to take the class, Erika only responded in a very quiet voice: "Yes ma'am," she said. The judge told her that if she didn't have the class completed by the next time she was scheduled to be in court, she would go to jail.

I was furious by how Erika had just been treated. I thought about Erika and her kids for the rest of the day. I thought about how, if situations and circumstances were different, I could be Erika. I could have been the one standing in court beside a lawyer, with my head hung in shame, as a judge yelled at me for not taking a class—all because I was too poor to do so. I became so emotional thinking about this—thinking about Erika—that I had to stop at my car in the garage to gather myself before heading back to my office from court.

Unlike my white colleagues, I couldn't pick up this job—and the issues that came along with it—at 8:00 a.m. and put it down at 5:00 p.m., when the day was over. I didn't have the privilege of hoping and believing that everything would be okay. And I sure as hell didn't have the privilege of choosing whether or not to discuss race. Too many of my white colleagues were uncomfortable talking about race and said they didn't see color, without understanding that by saying this, they were ignoring the very essence of who we are as Black people—and everything that we've lived, felt, and experienced, simply because of the color of our skin. Some thought race was a social justice issue that shouldn't be brought up in court, without understanding that if race wasn't brought up in the courtroom, where it mattered most, the system would never change.

I knew no one there would understand, and there was really no one to talk to about what I was feeling. Being a Black woman, I felt the office wasn't a safe space to discuss what I was seeing in the courtroom, in the community—or on the news for that matter—and how all of that may be impacting me. There was no one I could talk to about the grief I felt because of the systemic inequalities in the criminal justice system and the fact that it was never designed to work in our favor. There was no space to discuss what it was like to see a young Black man sentenced to life after his young white attorney put in no effort whatsoever to advocate on his behalf. And then, feeling yourself avoiding eye contact with his crying family afterward, because you know too well how his incarceration will impact not only him but his entire family. How his two sons, who were present in the courtroom, will now grow up without their father—in the same way that their father grew up without his. Knowing that these sons will likely experience a number of challenges and difficulties, including criminal activity. Knowing that the cycle will continue.

Knowing all of this but also understanding that not even for one second are you allowed to fully give in and acknowledge the realities of what is going on right in front of you. Because I knew if I did, the pain of what I was seeing would break me open, and I would never be able to stop crying. That once it began flowing, I would cry the tears I never cried in Alderson for the years and the hopes and the chances the system had taken from me. For the pain I saw every day in the faces of my clients and their families; for the despair and resignation I'd seen so many times in my clients' eyes as they signed away their lives to a plea bargain, knowing—even if they were innocent—that the prosecutor and the judge would punish them with harsher prosecution and a stiffer sentence for daring to challenge the system.

Nor was there space to discuss what it was like having the DAs automatically offer your white clients with addiction issues treatment, but offer your Black clients with addiction issues a sentence to serve in jail. Knowing that this racial disparity was the result of the failed War on Drugs, brought about because of the crack epidemic in the 1980s, and that it was only when white people started getting addicted to heroin that the narrative around combatting the problem changed from a punitive one to a more rehabilitative one. Only to be called "difficult," "trouble," or "angry" for pointing out the DAs' explicit biases because they didn't see the value in my Black clients' lives.

There was no safe space to discuss any of these things—not what it meant to be Black in the criminal justice system, nor what it meant to be a Black woman working in the criminal justice system. And *definitely* not what it meant to be a Black woman with a conviction on her record—someone who has personally experienced being torn down by this system, but who refused to let the system win. Someone who fought back against all odds, only to now have to carry the weight of having to be three times as good as everyone else.

It's a hell of a burden to carry, and I was tired. . . . Tired of fighting the system, tired of fighting the judges, tired of fighting the prosecutors and police officers, and tired of fighting for my own existence. There were several days that the weight of the system—upheld by white supremacist ideologies that are responsible for the present state of the criminal justice system—definitely took its toll on me.

But I knew I had to keep fighting. For myself, for the women from Alderson, and for my clients. But some days I didn't know where I would get the strength to carry on.

———

DURING ONE OF THESE PARTICULARLY HARD DAYS, I REMEMBER WALKING from court with my colleague Daniel, complaining about the injustices in the criminal legal system, as we so often did. But this day was different. Court had been exceptionally rough, and I was beyond tired—I was weary. Daniel and I were really good friends, and he knew I had started to feel as if the work I was doing just wasn't enough.

We had talked about feeling like I was on a hamster wheel, constantly going around and around, without anything really changing. Daniel and I talked about how the system was rooted in racism and that we attorneys at the office had an obligation to speak out about it. And if we, at the office, did not speak up, then we were contributing to the problem.

"So, what are you going to do about it? What's your next move?" Daniel asked as we walked. I had thought about that question for some time. There was an unrest in me, in my spirit, and I knew I had to do something. What, I wasn't sure, but I would know it when I saw it. I thought it may be policy work of some kind, but I just didn't know. What I did know was that I couldn't keep working in a system that devalued the very essence of who my clients were as Black people.

Daniel waited in silence as I pondered my answer. With tears in my eyes, I simply said, "I want my next position to be one where I am able to help my clients on a larger scale than what I am able to do now."

But what that looked like? I had no idea.

chapter 24

I CARRIED THIS FEELING WITH ME FOR MONTHS.

Then, one afternoon during the spring of 2019, I got together with two of my friends, Dawn and Gicola. Dawn was the executive director of Free Hearts, a nonprofit organization led by formerly incarcerated women, with the specific aim of providing support, education, and advocacy for families impacted by incarceration. And Gicola was the organization's statewide organizer. I had been volunteering with Free Hearts for a while and admired both Dawn and Gicola immensely.

The three of us met over lunch to catch up, talking about the work we all do—politics, organizing, advocacy—and somehow we got around to the subject of Washington, DC. I told them that it was my spirit city. "Every time I go to DC to visit one of my best friends, if I can't get a pass to tour the Capitol building, I at least have to go by and take pictures of it," I told them, pulling out my phone. It was filled with photos of the building, taken over the years. "I just feel like I'm supposed to be there," I said. But in what capacity, I didn't know.

"You know what, I'm going to give Justice Democrats your number, Keeda—they should really talk to you," Gicola responded. Justice Democrats, she explained, was a political action committee formed in response to Donald Trump's 2016 presidential election, devoted to getting more progressive Democratic candidates into Congress. "You're a lawyer, you're formerly incarcerated—you'd be the perfect person to run for Congress. Seriously." I could see the excitement building in Gicola's face. Dawn nodded along enthusiastically, agreeing: "Yeah, sis! You'd be great."

"*Congress?*" I repeated. "Girl, please." *Congress, Senate*—those things seemed like they belonged to another world. I didn't know many people who grew up saying they wanted to be congressmen and congresswomen or senators—particularly Black people. The thought had never, ever crossed my mind. But Gicola was persistent. With Dawn's added encouragement, they persuaded me to have a conversation with Justice Democrats and just see what they had to say.

A couple of weeks later, I was on the phone with one of their organizers, hearing more about their work. The organization's strategy was to recruit and support prospective congressional candidates by helping them run primary races against out-of-touch Democratic incumbents. Jim Cooper, our existing US representative for Tennessee's Fifth Congressional District (based in Nashville), had been serving in the position relatively unopposed since 2003. A few years back, I had written a letter to Cooper, offering to volunteer with him to work on criminal justice reform. I had been thinking about ways to abolish mandatory minimum sentencing laws, improve the reentry process for formerly incarcerated people, fix Tennessee's byzantine voter restoration process, and other ways he might be able to make the system equitable in a way that it had never been. We ended up meeting for fifteen minutes, after which I never heard from him again. The interaction with Cooper was disappointing. I knew that he had a reputation for being a moderate Democrat, at best; for not going far enough to fight for the communities that needed it most. Still, I didn't know if I was the person to take him to task.

I continued speaking with Justice Democrats while Gicola and Dawn nudged me forward. "This could be great, Keeda—you can do this!" they would say to me every time I mentioned that I'd just had another phone call with one of the organization's staff. Gicola encouraged me to watch *Knock Down the House*, a documentary that followed the 2018 primary campaigns of four progressive women candidates endorsed by Justice Democrats: Paula Jean Swearengin from West Virginia, Amy Vilela from Nevada, Cori Bush from Missouri, and Alexandria Ocasio-Cortez from New York.

It was motivating to see these women challenge the status quo in their respective races, unafraid to advocate fiercely for the issues affecting their communities most. I thought about other women who'd run similar races, both recently and in the past. Unapologetic Black women like Barbara Lee, congresswoman from California, who worked on the political campaigns for Black Panther Party cofounder Bobby Seale, as well as Shirley Chisholm, the first Black woman ever elected to Congress in 1969, and the first of us to run for a major party's presidential nomination in 1972. Since Lee's election in 1998, she's spent her decades-long career advocating for issues like affordable housing accessibility, decriminalizing marijuana, and other justice efforts aimed at dismantling the racist War on Drugs.

There were also the other women of color who ran successful congressional campaigns in 2018, who were not included in *Knock Down the House*, like Ayanna Pressley, Ilhan Omar, and Rashida Tlaib. I loved that every bit of work Ayanna did was deeply reflective of her community and what their needs really were. The legislation that she was putting forth stemmed directly from that intimate knowledge, from those years of being in dialogue with the people she was committed to serve. Plus, having a husband who was formerly incarcerated, understanding more than most what that means, she brought the issues affecting our community front and center. And Rashida's story was incredibly inspiring too. Reading and hearing her talk about feeling discredited and disrespected, having doors shut in her face as a Muslim woman running for public office—and still persisting—made me think of my own journey.

Justice Democrats ultimately decided not to support me. Regardless, I was determined to move forward—with or without them. The seed had been planted.

Dawn, Gicola, and I started talking more seriously about what running for Congress might actually look like. At the same time, people around Nashville began to get word that challengers for Jim Cooper were out there and that I might be one of them. Dawn had mentioned it to Andrea James, a colleague of hers I'd met a couple of times, who founded the National Council for Incarcerated and Formerly Incarcerated Women and Girls—another formerly incarcerated Black woman herself, doing amazing work. The next time Andrea and I met, she immediately expressed her enthusiasm over my potential run. "We need your voice," she told me. She asked if I'd ever attended Netroots Nation, an annual political convention for progressive political activists held in different cities each year. When I told her that no, I hadn't—I didn't even know what it was—she paid for me to go, right there on the spot. "This is important," she'd said.

I did go, and attended panels filled with Black thought-leaders from their communities—like self-proclaimed "hell-raising humanitarian" and former Ohio state senator Nina Turner; and Yvette Simpson, CEO of the progressive political action committee Democracy for

America. It was amazing to be around so many like-minded people doing inspiring work.

Left and right people began reaching out to me like Andrea did, putting their support behind me—believing in me—before I knew myself whether or not I would actually run.

Should I do this? Or should I not? Do I really want to take this on? Dawn and Gicola had already committed themselves to being my A-Team, doing whatever they could for me to make a campaign happen. Now, it was just up to me to make up my mind. For weeks, I went back and forth, balancing one set of factors against another. For one, I couldn't just quit my job and run for office. I had recently bought a house—I had a mortgage and bills to pay. But I was also at a point in my life where I could really live my life: relax, go to brunch, hang out with my family, go on vacation. For so long, I had been playing catchup. I spent nearly four years of my life in prison, and I dedicated almost every day since I left Alderson to making up for all that time lost.

I was in a good place and that very well might be turned upside down if I chose this path.

All of the hesitancy I had around running because of the bills I needed to pay and the income I needed to survive—these were all things that often kept the average person from running for office. But, I thought, it's exactly the "average person" who needs to run. People who *understand* the issues, not because they have been told about them, or learned about them through articles and reports, but because they've lived them personally.

But as I continued to work through all of these questions in my head, I kept coming back to one thing: running for Congress would allow me to represent my clients—and my community—on a larger scale than I was able to do as a public defender. Becoming a congresswoman would ultimately be a continuation of my advocacy for them, just not in the courtroom. What better way to meet my clients' needs than to be in a position to make laws around the very things we had been advocating for.

Everything in me said I needed to do this. Was it going to push me? Yes. Was it going to stretch me? Yes. But working in the Public Defender's Office pushed and stretched me too. And I did what I had to in order to meet a need. In order to serve people.

In running for Congress, I would strive to meet that need once again.

———

AT THE END OF THE SUMMER OF 2019, JUST A FEW SHORT MONTHS after that lunch with Gicola and Dawn that set everything in motion, I told the Public Defender's Office that I was planning to run for Congress. The plan was to make the announcement in October, then spend the next ten months campaigning until the election in August 2020.

During this time, I started working on getting a team together. I called several known political firms in Nashville, but they didn't return my calls. After several rounds of this, I was eventually told that no one in Nashville would be willing to work with me because I was primarying an incumbent. I was told that they didn't want to be blackballed or ostracized by Jim Cooper and the Democratic Party. Hearing this message repeated over and over again, it was becoming apparent why organizations like Justice Democrats were formed and necessary when challenging the status quo.

With no team in place because no one was willing to work with me, the planned October announcement didn't happen. Eventually, I did find a fundraiser willing to help with the campaign, but I had to go out of state to find her. Keisha, the woman I hired, was based in Atlanta.

I later received a detailed memo from my office, stating that if I chose to run for Congress, I would have to take a leave of absence from the office starting January 2020. It was an impossible scenario. I had all the normal bills that everyone else has. I wasn't from a wealthy family that could cover my expenses. I was your everyday, average person with everyday, average person bills. So, taking an un-paid leave of absence for eight months just wasn't something I could do. I had to have a job.

I met with Gicola and Dawn to deliver the bad news. I told them we had no choice but to postpone the campaign until 2022, to give me enough time to save money and find a new job that would pro-vide more flexibility to run. I then reached out to Keisha as well, and, reluctantly, we agreed to put things on hold. Everyone was disappointed.

But later that evening, Dawn sent a group text to me and Gicola: "Keeda, you're running for Congress. You can come work with us at Free Hearts—we need an attorney."

Feeling a resurgence of hope, the next day Dawn and I spoke about the details. Transitioning to a nonprofit, I was worried that I still might have to work two jobs to make up the difference to cover all of my bills. "We'll match your current salary," Dawn responded when I expressed my concerns. "And we'll give you full benefits and a 401(k) with a match too. Start whenever you want."

I couldn't believe it. In the span of less than twenty-four hours, I went from resigning to the reality that a campaign would not be pos-sible at this time, to having a job with the flexibility I needed to run.

I called Keisha to give her the latest update: "Okay," she responded, excited. "We're back on."

Just like that—because of the support and belief coming from those around me—I was going to be able to get into the race. You couldn't tell me that I wasn't in this because God wanted me to be. He had never ceased to prove that He would make a way.

The next few days I pondered what not being a public defender would look like. While I knew I would never be a career public defender, it was still the reason I went to law school in the first place. I thought of my clients, and how leaving them in the hands of others would be the hardest thing to do.

It wasn't just my clients who were subjected to the double standards of the criminal justice system—so were the lawyers. Those of us who are assertive or confident are often viewed as less likable, by both men and women. And then you add in the stereotypes of "angry" and "unfriendly" for Black women, and you have all the makings of a tense work environment, to say the least.

Several times in court, I was labeled as the "Angry Black Woman" by judges and district attorneys for standing up and advocating for my clients, while my white counterparts who made the same arguments were simply seen as "vigorously advocating" for their clients. Never once was a white attorney ever considered "extra" or "trouble" because they dared question the DA about an unfair offer that they made to a client or because they had dared to question the ruling of a judge. Day in and day out, this was my reality.

Being a Black female attorney means that you have to be twice as good as your white colleagues: one, because you are Black; and two, because you're a woman. But for me, it didn't end there. Several white women attorneys questioned my hiring at the Public Defender's Office because I didn't go to a top-tier law school, as they had, and because I was a "felon" (in their words). Once, a judge questioned my integrity, in open court, in front of my clients and the district attorneys.

I endured all of these things, and more, simply because I was formerly incarcerated. So, while Black women have to be twice as good in the workplace, when you factor being formerly incarcerated into that equation, I had to be three times as good. And that's another huge burden to carry.

My ideas were often ignored, or taken and implemented by others without giving me credit for them. My successes weren't celebrated in the same manner as everyone else's. I felt like I was only being tolerated as the token "formerly incarcerated lawyer" to give some type of credence that the office believed in second chances. Over time, I stopped engaging. And then, not only was I the Angry Black Woman, but I was also not a team player.

And so, no, I would definitely not miss the double standards among my colleagues or the double standards within the system itself. But my clients, I would miss a lot. I may not have been the best public defender, and I definitely made mistakes along the way, but I always tried to treat my clients with the dignity and respect that they deserved. Several of my clients, I grew very close with throughout my representation of them and beyond. Those were the ones that I called my "special" clients. I visited them in treatment; I held their hand in the hospital while they went through withdrawal from heroin; I picked them up for court; and I answered my phone at very late hours for them when they just needed someone to talk to.

One day after visiting a client's mom—who called me just as much as her son, my client, did—the investigator with me asked if I had known the family before I started representing him. "No, why?" I asked. She said that the way that I dealt with him and his entire family, one would have thought that I knew them personally. "I've never seen any of the other lawyers I work with have the kind of relationships you have with most of your clients, Keeda," she commented. "That's what being client-centered is all about."

As my final days in the office counted down, I reminisced about my time there, and some of the clients I'd met over the years. I thought about Ms. Jenkins, who had written me a letter from treatment, thanking me for caring enough about her to make sure she got the support she needed to live a sober life. I thought about Devontea, who said that he had never had a public defender fight for him like I had. I thought about Lamont, who teared up because he thought he let me down when he violated his probation; and Michelle, who only needed someone to believe in her, that she could be something other than a prostitute. I thought of Dartrell, who always called me his girlfriend while simultaneously asking me for a dollar. And I thought about Freddie.

Freddie was a white guy in his late twenties when I first represented him on a domestic violence charge. His hair was dark and cut short, and he had tattoos up and down both of his arms. He was no taller than I was and very mild-mannered. Although Freddie and I were as different as night and day, we got along well. As with so many of my other clients, Freddie and I became friends. So, when he was arrested a few times after we first met, I always represented him. The last time that he was released, he promised me that he wasn't coming back to jail. "I'm going to get my life together," he said. And he did. When I called him to tell him that I was leaving the Public Defender's Office, he was so excited. We talked for several minutes, catching up, and at the end of the call, overcome with emotion, he told me that he appreciated everything that I had ever done for him. He said that no lawyer had ever fought for him like I had and that I had become more than just a lawyer. I was family. The same way that Freddie considered me family, each of my clients was like family to me. They are who I would miss. And it was them who I would always continue to fight for.

I would stay at the office for the next month to allow enough time to talk to my clients about the decision I was making and to let them know that their cases would be assigned to other attorneys.

CHAPTER 24

And then, on December 19, 2019, at 4:30 p.m., after a typical long day—with no lunch, fighting with a judge in court about one of my clients to the very end—I logged off my computer, said my few goodbyes, and turned in my badge. After six and a half years, I closed my office door for the last time. While I would no longer be employed as a public defender, I would always be one at heart.

———

WE WOULD OFFICIALLY ANNOUNCE MY CANDIDACY FOR CONGRESS ON the first Monday after the new year: January 6, 2020. And we would do it with only a single fundraiser and a few volunteers, since no one in Nashville was willing to help with our campaign.

In that two-week period between my final day at the Public Defender's Office and our official announcement, a lot of things needed to be done. Keisha, my fundraiser from Atlanta, had gotten the ball rolling: setting up accounts, constructing a splash page for my website. Throughout the entirety of that holiday break, I worked with her to get everything together. This was the beginning of a lot of sleepless nights.

And then once January 6 came around, we hit the ground running.

Our strategy was to launch the campaign on social media first, then spend a couple of months fundraising and do the big kickoff event in March. We secured the event at a space called the Lab in Nashville and started planning the details. We also made plans to hold a fundraiser in Franklin at the end of the month to allow people from my hometown to donate and be part of the campaign.

But then, March 2020 arrived and with it the entire city—and eventually the entire world—changed.

The campaign kickoff event was scheduled for March 10. But late into March 2, through the morning hours of March 3, a tornado blew through Middle Tennessee, decimating the Lab in its path.

Two of the major areas impacted were north and east Nashville, both parts of the city where Black people predominantly lived. Many of those who lost their houses didn't have homeowner's insurance or were underinsured. Whole neighborhoods were leveled. Because so many people were impacted, it seemed completely inappropriate to continue to fundraise. And so, against my fundraiser's wishes, I decided to suspend my campaign for a month to help with cleanup and donations.

Throughout the month I helped in the efforts to put our city back together again. I picked up debris in north and east Nashville. I donated boxes and several other items. Because of the damage done to so many homes, a lot of the homeowners had legal questions, and so I volunteered with the Legal Aid Society of Middle Tennessee to provide legal assistance.

But then, of course—immediately on the heels of the tornado—COVID-19 came. As all the major cities across the country—New York, Atlanta, and so many others—began to shut down, the standard rulebook for how campaigns were run started to change, virtually overnight. For almost two weeks after the virus arrived on the scene, our campaign came to a complete standstill, as people across the political landscape struggled to figure out what the coronavirus was and how to navigate through it in uncharted terrain. Emails came flooding in with subject lines: *How to Fundraise during COVID-19; How to Convert Your Campaign to a Digital Campaign; How to Do Your Kickoffs via Zoom; How to Build Digital Engagement.* Clearly, the future would look very different now. But how different—and for how long—nobody truly knew.

And in the midst of it all, I still had to fundraise. Not many candidates like to do this, and it was definitely my least favorite part of campaigning. And factoring in the tornado and the pandemic on top of this, I was super uncomfortable asking people for money when they didn't even know if they were going to have a job from one day to the next. To help deal with these issues, my team thought it was best to hire new fundraising people who were more familiar with the politics in Tennessee. Because of COVID this was not campaigning as usual. There were no in-person events, so we couldn't meet people. There was no door knocking. Everything had moved online. And so, I participated in as many Zoom panels as I could—sometimes five to six a week. We did what we could to meet constituents in our district, but it was challenging when we couldn't see people face-to-face. But we continued on.

Because we didn't have a lot of money starting off, and we hadn't raised a lot of money, I put in some of my own. I also conducted the research for my campaign issues by myself. Many nights, I stayed up until 4 a.m., gathering the information that formed the basis of our platform. Criminal justice reform, of course, was the centerpiece, with repealing mandatory minimum sentencing laws and promoting voter restoration rights at the top of my list. Health care and economic justice, immigration and gender justice, environmental and climate justice all rounded out the rest—issues I had intimate knowledge of in some capacity, either through my years advocating for clients in the Public Defender's Office and for people within my community or by experiencing them firsthand.

Before the coronavirus, our original plan was to do various listening tours throughout the community, so that people could talk about the issues that were most important to them. The issues that affected people most in Nashville were the same ones impacting people countrywide. And the virus, we would soon learn, exacerbated them all. As always, those without suffered more. And people of color suffered the most. Almost in real time, as the pandemic was unfolding, we could *see* how the virus was ravaging communities based on race, based on economic status, because of a lack of health care. We could see how people in jails and prisons were left unprotected in their facilities—how Black people in the prison system, especially, were left behind as policies to release certain "low-risk" prisoners to alleviate crowding overwhelmingly disfavored them. Only 7 percent of Black men in the federal system could be deemed low-risk enough for COVID-19 release, according to the government's metrics, versus 30 percent of white men.

Clearly, the issues in my campaign were urgent. The world continued to confirm that fact as each day passed.

During this same period of time—between the tornado, and the pandemic, and the launch of my campaign—I got my civil rights reinstated. Although I had previously regained my voting rights, this allowed me the right to sit on a jury and to hold state public office, among other things. Peter became my attorney once again and filed the motion in Circuit Court and represented me at the hearing. Neither the local District Attorney's Office nor the US Attorney's Office objected to the restoration of my rights—they were not even present at the hearing. After hearing my testimony about all of the things that I had accomplished since leaving Alderson, the judge, Kelvin Jones, granted my motion.

It was the final culmination of my case. The most I could be granted short of an official pardon. I could have run for Congress with or without my civil rights, but with them, I felt that much more motivated in my mission to continue the work of creating a second-chance culture so other formerly incarcerated and justice-impacted individuals could have the same opportunities I had been afforded throughout my reentry process.

———

SLOWLY, WE STARTED TO GET THE CAMPAIGN BACK ON TRACK. I HIRED A few more people to the team and settled into the routine of making fundraising calls. Being COVID-conscious, we had volunteers spread the word by putting campaign literature on people's doors since we couldn't do the traditional door knocking. We also had volunteers doing phone banking and texting. We handed out yard signs. And we put up thirty huge signs all over Nashville featuring my picture with "Keeda Haynes for Congress" printed in big, bold lettering.

The response from the community was generally positive—a lot of people were genuinely excited by the prospect of real, over-due change. Some people said Jim Cooper was just there taking up space, and they were glad I was running. "He needs to go—he hasn't done anything for us," I'd hear. Others, however, were more skepti-cal, questioning why I was running against the incumbent. "What makes you think you have the experience?"; "Now's not the time to run against Jim Cooper"; "Nashville's not New York." And for some, Cooper was simply the option they'd grown accustomed to over the years. He was what people knew.

Cooper and his family had embedded themselves into the power structure of our state for decades. His father, Prentice Cooper, was the governor of Tennessee from 1939 to 1945. (He ran on a segre-gationist platform that produced policies and procedures that Black people are still trying to recover from, decades later.) His grandfather, William Prentice Cooper, was Speaker of the Tennessee House of Representatives. And his brother, John Cooper, has been the mayor of Nashville since 2019.

In running against Jim Cooper, we were fundamentally challeng-ing the status quo. By doing that, we were also challenging the entire network of power that came along with it. And some people did not like having their power challenged. "How dare she run for Congress," I heard people say about my campaign. "She's never held office before. If she wants to do this, she should start in local politics first." Jim Coo-per, mind you, had never been involved in local politics. Before first running for Congress in the Fourth District in the 1980s, Cooper had spent a short time working as an attorney in a private law firm. Compared to my six and a half *years* as an attorney, working in the trenches in the Public Defender's Office.

Other people would ask me: "Well, what's your platform? What are you going to do when you get to Congress?" and expected me to respond with a fully fleshed out, comprehensive legislative agenda—including how the government was going to pay for it—every single time I opened my mouth. Still others told me they wanted to see how much money I raised before they agreed to support me: "That way we know you're for real." Or they might say, "I do plan to vote for you—but I'm not going to publicly say it." The strategy was that people didn't know whether I actually had a chance to win, and they wanted to keep their relationship with the Coopers just in case I didn't.

But this is what it looks like when people of color and women are held to a different standard than white men. This is what it looks like when the walls to accessing power are high. In my campaign—as for us everywhere—the inequal barriers to entry just to play the game were very, very real.

Just as in our search for fundraisers, local media would barely touch us. My friends volunteering with the campaign reached out to several news outlets, but they all either declined, or we heard nothing back from them at all. These same outlets covered the Senate race and even had the Republican candidate on one of their shows but never even discussed the congressional race that I was in. It was obvious not only that it was a problem that I was running against Jim Cooper but also that the Establishment was fine with the status quo.

We did receive a couple of write-ups, including one in the *Nashville Scene* and a few other outlets. But other than that, crickets. One single local news station did reach out toward the very end of the campaign, but I only had about ninety seconds of airtime to answer one question on their morning show, then the recording was done.

While the local media and some local politicians would not touch us, there were some that were supportive from the very beginning—particularly a few Black women who'd been working fiercely on behalf of our people for years. State Senator Brenda Gilmore, a champion for the Black community in all of her political efforts, was one of the first people to endorse me. After I announced my candidacy, she reached out—not to tell me what I was doing wrong, like some others, but to ask what she could do to help. She made sure to share our campaign information on social media, she held forums, and she even worked polls—wearing a "Keeda Haynes for Congress" shirt. "Keeda Haynes is a leader that will fight for causes and issues that will deliver the reforms that we need," she said when she publicly announced her endorsement. "She will be the voice that we need during these challenging times." Senator Gilmore's unwavering support, even in the face of the status quo, showed that she believed in what this campaign stood for—and that she believed in me.

Community thought-leader Phyllis Hildreth believed in me too. I met Phyllis a few years back when we were both doing community work, and we kept in touch over the years. The words she used to endorse me, that my "training, knowledge, experience and grounding in community" equipped me to "answer the call and do the work justice demands" meant a lot coming from someone whom I had respected and admired for so long.

We also received endorsements from then-presidential candidate Marianne Williamson, prominent civil rights attorney Abby Rubenfeld, former Tennessee State Senate candidate Wade Munday, and Metro Nashville Councilmembers Sean Parker and Emily Benedict—who, even without having personally met me, still believed in our campaign's message and that I was the best person to represent our district in Congress.

On the national level, several progressive political organizations like Democracy for America, Our Revolution, Sunrise Movement, and Indivisible gave endorsements early on. They also donated to my campaign, volunteered at polling locations, held phone banks, did lit drops, and so many other things to help support our work. I would not have been able to do some of the things that we did in the campaign without their support from the beginning. From there, the endorsements continued to roll in. Political action committees like the Collective PAC, devoted to fixing the underrepresentation of Black people in elected seats of power across the country; Blue America, aimed at replacing conservatives in Congress with progressives dedicated to serving the needs of ordinary Americans; and the Progressive Change Campaign Committee, a million-member grassroots organization that had backed candidates like Elizabeth Warren, Ilhan Omar, and Alexandria Ocasio-Cortez during their various campaigns, also put their support behind us.

And then, on May 25, 2020, once again, our campaign took an unexpected turn, when George Floyd was murdered on video by a white police officer, who pressed his knee onto Floyd's neck as he cried, "I can't breathe." But there was also Breonna Taylor, Ahmaud Arbery, and so many other Black people who had been killed at the hands of police or white vigilantes. Including Jocques Clemmons, Daniel Hambrick, and William Johnson Jr., who had all been killed right here in Nashville by white police officers. There was blood on the ground in the streets of Nashville as well.

Each of their stories was different, but they all had one thing in common: a criminal justice system that too often disrespected and devalued the lives of Black people—something I had seen time and time again working as a public defender for the past six and a half years.

And so, in the middle of a pandemic, masked up, we took our campaign to the streets. Like everyone else across the country, I held up my Black Lives Matter sign and marched in the streets to protest the unjust killing of Black people in this country. It was clear that the uprising, spurred by this recent spree of racially charged police killings, on a deeper level was a response to centuries of systemic racism and hate inflicted on us and our communities—both in Nashville and across the country.

Black people have been beaten, brutalized, disrespected, and murdered for the last four hundred years in America. And even today, at the hands of the police, this violence continues. When we marched, we were saddened, angry, frustrated, and fed up. No longer could we sit on the sidelines accepting empty platitudes from our elected officials, quoting Martin Luther King Jr. at us about peace, while taking money from defense companies that have aided in the militarization of the very police that are hunting us down and killing us.

During that summer of 2020, it was apparent that to see the change we were all demanding, we would have to choose between leaders who were comfortable with the status quo, only acting when pushed, or electing people who not only understood the cost of systemic racism but would fight to dismantle it. I was ready to lead the efforts in Congress to truly make sure that Black lives mattered in our district and in our country.

Suddenly, on a global scale, the criminal justice system was being called into question. The social justice issues running throughout my platform were alive, every day, in the streets. And my story, both as a victim of the criminal justice system and as an advocate for its reform, started making the news. I did virtual panels with Ayanna Pressley and Rashida Tlaib—the same women politicians I'd admired from afar when I first started entertaining the idea of running for Congress. There were articles about my campaign featured on CNN and ABC News, the *Huffington Post*, CNBC, and Black media powerhouses including Essence, BET, and Black Enterprise.

"'Black Lives Matter' can't just be a chant we say when we're out in the streets protesting," I often said during interviews and on panels. "A lot of these discriminatory laws are codified—from redlining to the education system to mass incarceration. Which is why we need lawmakers from underrepresented communities that can view these policies and procedures from our lens. Lawmakers that will advance an agenda that will promote and protect the true liberation of Black people to create the justice and healing that our communities need. Black lives have to matter when it comes to education. Black lives have to matter when it comes to voting rights. Black lives have to matter when it comes to housing. Black lives have to matter when it comes to jobs. Black lives have to matter when it comes to infrastructure. Black lives have to matter when it comes to the environment. We need to ensure that Black lives matter across every single aspect of our society. As a former public defender, I've fought these discriminatory policies every day for the past six and a half years. This is nothing new to me. This is personal."

And it was.

———

WE FOUGHT HARD. BUT IN THE END—EVEN WITH THE HEIGHTENED national media focus—ultimately it wasn't enough. When the results were tabulated after the August 6, 2020, election, the status quo had won. But we gave Jim Cooper a hell of a run for his money. We captured nearly 40 percent of the vote.

Some people said, had we had another month, the results may have turned out differently. That I had just run out of time. Because by the time people had really found out who I was, it was too late.

CHAPTER 24

"You need to run again," they said. "People were excited," they said. "You built so much momentum."

People *were* genuinely excited. No, I didn't win—but there were Tennesseans casting their ballots who had never voted in the primary before. I remember going into the mall a few days after the campaign, and as I was checking out at a store, a few women approached me. "Are you Keeda?" they asked. I told them I was, and they said how proud they were of me. "We voted for you!" they all said, excitedly. One of the women even mentioned that she got her voting rights reinstated just so she could cast her ballot for me. "It's so nice to see someone we can relate to running for office," they said. As we said our goodbyes, they encouraged me to run again.

There were other formerly incarcerated people I heard from who wanted to get their voting rights reinstated as a result of my campaign, because for once there was someone on the ballot they were excited to vote for. People told me that I made them realize the importance of voting in all elections. Every time. Mothers sent me pictures of their young daughters standing proudly beside my campaign sign. Former clients reached out to say that even though they couldn't compensate me for my services when I represented them as a public defender, they were going to support me in the election—that their vote was how they would repay me. Once, a young Black woman—eighteen, nineteen years old—came by my table with her family while I was in the middle of brunch at a restaurant, just to tell me it was her first time voting in a congressional race. "And I was so proud that I had the option to vote for someone who looked like me."

Those types of things were the wins. Those things made it all worth it. They spoke louder than any of the critics ever could.

We are experiencing the tide changing. People are tired of wealthy white men representing us, leading the conversation. It's true that

Tennessee is a little slower to change than other places, but we *are* seeing people standing up to the status quo. Saying the status quo is no longer sufficient. Saying, "Thank you for your service, but you no longer serve us. You do not speak for us. You do not understand our issues." The year 2020 saw the highest-ever number of women in history running for Congress around the country. There were 583 of us who submitted our names for House races—including at least 130 Black women. I hope by the time this book is published, those numbers will have climbed up even more.

But while the country is shifting, there is still a need to keep moving from the thought of more diverse leadership—to the reality of it. From the thought of more women, and people of color, and Black women taking the reins—to the potent, powerful reality of it.

This is especially true for those of us who have been formerly incarcerated. For us, the void in leadership is even more deeply felt. We say we believe in second chances. We say that we want people with criminal records to be reintegrated into society and not live as second-class citizens. But how far do those chances extend? What is the limit?

Those of us who have been impacted by the criminal justice system must have a meaningful say in making legislation that's going to directly impact us. Our voices, our ideas, our stories must be heard.

There's a saying in our community: "Nothing for us, without us."

The fight for our seat at the table continues. And I'm ready to carry on.

epilogue

"THE ARC OF THE MORAL UNIVERSE IS LONG, BUT IT BENDS TO-wards justice."

It's one of Martin Luther King Jr.'s most famous quotes—uttered during his rousing speech, "How Long? Not Long!" given at the conclusion of the 1965 civil rights march from Selma to Montgomery, Alabama.

I'm sure that many of us have heard the phrase used in some manner or another over the years as a way to rally hope, strengthen conviction, encourage people to stay in whatever fight they've committed themselves to. Former president Barack Obama invoked the words often in his own speeches; he even had them woven into a rug in the Oval Office. And rightfully so: Obama knew, I think, that real justice—significant changes to the systemic inequities we face—would not come about in one single moment. Nor, as history has clearly shown us, would it simply arrive with the passage of time as an inevitable conclusion, an automatic guarantee.

Because while the arc of the moral universe may bend toward justice—*nothing* bends without us first bending it.

If the arc automatically bent toward justice, my own story would look very different. My life would have never been turned upside down by a wrongful conviction. Nor would I have ever gone to prison. Instead, like so many on the receiving end of an inherently unfair system, justice for me was something I had to fight for. A thing I could get—for myself, and later for my clients—only by challenging the oppressive forces around me.

Achieving real justice requires applying constant pressure. And not just by a few well-intentioned individuals. Bending the arc will take a movement. A movement that reimagines justice by first acknowledging the humanity in people.

This is where the work must begin.

The current criminal legal system is structured around who is worthy and who is unworthy—who belongs and who does not. If we strip people of their dignity, their humanity, it's easier to think they're not the same as us. And if they're not the same as us, we don't have to sympathize. But there is humanity in everyone, no matter what they are alleged to have done. We are all more than the worst act we are alleged to have committed.

To create the kind of justice we want to see, as a society we must collectively think in new and different ways than we have in the past. We must take the time and care to see people as *people*—as the complex individuals they are. When we do this, we can begin to truly understand how they found themselves in the situations they're in. Or more accurately, we can begin to understand the systems that *created* their situations in the first place.

Real justice must envision a system where the pain and trauma of people's lives is met with healing and compassion, instead of punishment and cages. Where people in our communities are supported; where they can get what they need to be successful—however they measure that success. When we shift our focus this way, we *want* people to be taken care of. Because when we humanize people, what we're essentially asking is this: *What would I want for myself? For a family member? For a loved one or a close friend?*

The more time I spent navigating the criminal justice system—particularly as a public defender, getting to know the people it impacted—the more I realized how much it neglected the complex issues of the individuals caught inside. Day after day, year after year, I encountered people whose cases ended up on my desk as a result of multiple, often overlapping systems that had failed them: an educational system that routinely left them behind, ultimately funneling them into the school to prison pipeline; a mental health system that ignored their issues; an economic system that provided them no livable wage or the means to earn a wage. A health care system that denied them any available resources. I began thinking that these issues were all like branches of one massive, centuries-old tree. And systemic racism was the thick root that allowed that tree to live and to grow. You may be able to cut off one branch of the tree, but if you don't attack the root—digging it up entirely from where it lies—a new branch will inevitably regenerate in its place.

To address the problems within our existing systems, it is crucial to understand all the different ways these problems manifest. And now, more than ever before, important conversations are starting to be had.

But now that we've arrived at this moment, our greatest challenge will come with what we do next.

Bending the arc takes effort.

It takes action.

It takes pressure.

The work continues.

Author's Note

THIS BOOK INVOLVES PEOPLE AND SOME EVENTS THAT HAPPENED YEARS ago in my life. These events have been written to the best of my recollection. Out of respect for my former clients and the attorney-client relationship, names of my former clients have been changed, along with a few other names of people I encountered in the criminal legal system. No other names have been altered.

Acknowledgments

I WOULD LIKE TO FIRST THANK GOD FOR ALLOWING ME THE OPPORTU-
nity to share some of my experiences with the world in the hope
that they will inspire and encourage someone else along the way. I
also want to thank my family: my mother, Stephanie; my daddy, John;
my brothers, Prince, Tyke, and Johnathon; my sister, Anitra; my aunt
Shawn; my uncles Garfield, Ben, and Rod; my great aunts, Diane and
Sally (Tit); and the rest of my family for all of the love and support
they have given me, not just during this journey but throughout my
entire life. You all have been there for me in more ways than I can
count, and I would not be the woman that I am today without your
unwavering support. I love you all so much.

There were so many people who helped bring this book to life,
but I want to specifically thank Eric Schlosser. We met when you came
to Nashville to include me in your book about women in prisons but
immediately decided that I needed to tell my own story in my own
words. From that day forward you worked to make sure that would
happen and have been a great friend and sounding board throughout
this process. To my literary agent, Margaret Riley King, you believed

in me and my story from the day we met and have gone above and beyond to make this book happen. My editor, Emi Ikkanda, and the entire team at Seal Press, thank you for seeing the importance of my life story being told and for giving me the opportunity to do so. Many thanks to Maya Millett for jumping right in and putting up with me for months and months on end. You were extremely patient and understanding with me as I relived, again, some of the most tragic experiences in my life. You helped bring my thoughts to life. And to Evan Sutton for helping with some of the tough issues.

I have to give a special thank you to Peter Strianse. Peter, you were the best attorney anyone could have asked for, as well as a good friend. Thank you for believing in me and for never giving up on me. Not only did you have an impact on my life, but you impacted so many other clients whom I had the privilege of watching you represent. You really set the bar as to who a criminal defense attorney should be. I can never repay you for all of the things that you've done for me, but know that my family and I are truly grateful for "Cousin Peter."

To all of my friends, from the beginning to now, I thank you all for your love and support as each of you walked with me through various phases of my life. I love every one of you.

To all of my clients whom I represented at the Metro Nashville Public Defender's Office: Thank you for trusting in me and allowing me the opportunity to amplify your voices for those who do not always listen. You all taught me so much about myself and life in ways that you couldn't possibly imagine. You will forever be a part of my story and one of the reasons I continue to do the work that I do.

Last, but certainly not least, to all the women from Alderson Federal Prison Camp, all my formerly incarcerated and justice-impacted family: As we walk our individual roads in life, know that I am rooting for you. On the days, for whatever reason, you feel you can't go on, know that I am walking alongside you. And on the days when you experience victory, know that I am celebrating with you. I believe in you, and I believe that each of you has the courage, perseverance, and persistence it takes to walk in and fulfill your destiny. You too are living proof!

KEEDA J. HAYNES is a criminal justice reform advocate and a former public defender. She is the Voting Rights Campaign Strategist with the Sentencing Project. In 2020, she ran for Congress to represent Tennessee's Fifth District. She lives in Nashville, Tennessee.